Post-War Childhood

Post-War Childhood

Growing up in the not-so-friendly
'Baby Boomer' years

Simon Webb

PEN & SWORD
HISTORY

First published in Great Britain in 2017 by
PEN & SWORD HISTORY
an imprint of
Pen & Sword Books Ltd,
47 Church Street,
Barnsley,
South Yorkshire,
S70 2AS

A CIP record for this book is available from the British Library.

ISBN 978 1 47388 601 8

Printed and bound by Gutenberg Press Ltd., Malta.

Pen & Sword Books Ltd incorporates the Imprints of Pen & Sword Aviation,
Pen & Sword Maritime, Pen & Sword Military, Wharncliffe Local History,
Pen & Sword Select, Pen & Sword Military Classics and Leo Cooper.

For a complete list of Pen & Sword titles please contact
Pen & Sword Books Limited
47 Church Street, Barnsley, South Yorkshire, S70 2AS, England
E-mail: enquiries@pen-and-sword.co.uk
Website: www.pen-and-sword.co.uk

Contents

List of Plates

1. A road sign from the 1950s.

2. Boys trainspotting at a railway station.

3. A playground in 1950s Britain.

4. The playground rocking horse, cause of many serious injuries.

5. A 1957 advertisement for air rifles.

6. An open penknife.

7. A knife as a souvenir from the seaside.

8. An air pistol in the Webley catalogue.

9. Housewives cleaning their front steps in the 1950s.

10. Newspaper headlines from 1960 and 1964.

11. Children playing on a bomb site in the 1950s.

12. Children on a bomb site fool around with a pickaxe.

13. A remaining bomb site in London.

14. An iron lung.

15. A ward full of children in iron lungs.

Introduction

We are all of us familiar with old people who contend that when they were young, everything was a great improvement on the present day. Children in the past, for instance, were better behaved, healthier, more polite to, and respectful of, their elders, showed greater courage and resourcefulness, read more and generally had a higher level of educational attainment into the bargain. This type of false-memory syndrome has been a traditional affliction of the elderly since time out of mind. The latest generation to fall prey to such distorted views of the past is of course that of the so-called baby boomers; those born roughly between 1946 and 1964. Enormously entertaining though it is to observe the Flower Power children of the 1960s turning into querulous old men and women who complain that the country is going to the dogs and that childhood isn't a patch on it what it was when they were themselves youngsters, there is a more serious side to the matter.

The childhood years of the baby boomers have not only become the object of immense and unremitting nostalgia, but the practices and customs of those days as regards children are now being widely advocated as the perfect model of childhood. In newspapers, magazines, books and websites, the way of life for children in the 1950s is now viewed as a desirable pattern to follow. It is as though schooldays in the 1950s and 1960s have become universally accepted as some Platonic ideal of childhood; the yardstick and touchstone against which all other childhoods, especially those of today, are to be measured. If children are obese, it must be because they no longer walk to school and play out of doors as they did in the 1960s. That reading is no longer a popular pastime for children can only be because they spend all their time glued to electronic screens. There was nothing like that in the 1950s, and just think how much children used to read in those days! Are educational standards falling? Might this be remedied by getting children to chant their multiplication tables out loud as they did in the 1950s and perhaps altering schools until they are more like those of the post-war years? Or consider all the knife crime and gang warfare that we read about in the newspapers. In the decades following the end of the Second World War, youngsters were too busy playing Cowboys and Indians to even think of becoming feral youths. In those days, juvenile crime and disorder was unheard of, apart from playing knock-down-ginger on people's front doors or occasionally scrumping apples. Wouldn't it be marvellous if we could turn back the clock and make childhood once more a time of innocence, where children pursue such harmless and wholesome hobbies as stamp collecting and trainspotting?

Illustrations 1 and 2 sum up and encapsulate how many older people feel about baby boomer childhood. The first shows two children, neatly and appropriately dressed and obviously on their way to school, striding confidently across a road. This reminds us that in the 1950s and 1960s, it was the almost universal practice for young children to make their own way to school unescorted by adults, let alone driven there in a car. The second illustration shows a group of boys trainspotting at a mainline railway station in the 1950s. This photograph typifies for many the uncomplicated lifestyle of children in those days. Here are children who are not 'sexting' or accessing indecent or violent material on the Internet. If only modern children could spend more time outdoors in this way, engaged in such an innocuous pastime!

Nonsense of this kind about a past golden age of childhood would be harmless and amusing enough if it were limited to grandmothers reminiscing to young relatives about how the world was when they were at school, or were it to be found only in letters written to the newspapers which bemoan the behaviour of modern youth. What we are now seeing, though, are NHS trusts and government departments vying with each other to see who can be most zealous in praising the childhood enjoyed by the baby boomers and trying to come up with schemes to encourage children to emulate those days by walking to school, giving up television and computers in favour of books, playing out of doors more and eating a diet more like that of children sixty years ago, before the 'obesity crisis' began. Doctors, teachers and politicians are now acting as though childhood in the time of the baby boomers really *was* healthier, both physically and intellectually, than that experienced by British children of the twenty-first century.

Often, this longing for a vanished past is inextricably associated with the supposedly greater freedom which children enjoyed until as late as the 1970s, 'playing out' on their own and walking to school, without the supervision of adults. Little wonder that without all that exercise, they have grown flabby and overweight, just waiting to fall victim to Type 2 diabetes! This must also be why today's youth have not developed sturdy self-reliance; they spend all their time at home and never have the chance to learn about coping with minor emergencies or tricky situations without their parents hovering around, ready to step in and help them.

Here is a fairly typical example of the claims made about both the superiority of childhood in the past and also some of the probable ill effects for modern children of not experiencing a childhood similar to that of those born during the baby boomer years;

> Forgive the rant, but I fear for the sort of mollycoddled children we are raising today. Danger and risk are a part of life. Exposure to them helps us to judge and react to them. It builds our common sense. They are, I would argue, essential to growing up. We should allow our children to play in the streets, climb trees, walk to school, play down the park, cycle round the neighbourhood, go to the corner shop, etc. They will become better adults as a result.

This, at least, is what Steve Stack claims in his book *21st Century Dodos* and it is to be suspected that many adults who grew up in the 1950s, 1960s and 1970s would agree with him. Perhaps it would help to look briefly at the ideas which Stack propounds, and to which many of that generation subscribe, to see if there might be more to this than meets the eye.

We shall cover some of these things in greater detail later in this book, but let us consider for now just one or two of the suggestions which Stack makes, which he claims would create better adults. What about the idea that danger and risk are a part of life and that exposure to them helps us build our common sense? One often sees this idea expressed by older adults and it is invariably made by those who survived the risks and consequently lived to become better adults in later life. Not all children have been as fortunate. It is sometimes said that history is written by the victors and in the case of childhood reminiscences, the history is written by those who overcame the various risks which some of them now view in such a cavalier way.

Take, for example, the assertion made above that we should allow children to play in the streets and walk to school alone. A lot will be said of these two ideas later, but for now it is enough to note that in 1965, forty-five times as many children were killed by cars each year while walking alone to school and playing in the streets as are currently dying in this way. Or what about another hazard when walking to school unescorted by a parent or other adult, one which is seldom encountered by modern children? In 1965, the same year that almost a thousand child pedestrians were killed by traffic, a little girl of six set off to school alone in the Midlands. She was snatched from the street by a homicidal maniac and turned up dead in a ditch a few weeks later.

Other things which will evidently produce 'better adults' are apparently children playing in the park and going to the corner shop by themselves. Both activities can, and did in the 1960s, end in violent death. Here are two more children who did not grow up to be better adults as a result of these experiences; indeed, they did not make it to adulthood at all. Take the nine-year-old girl playing Cowboys and Indians in the local park and also an even younger boy visiting the corner shop alone.

In 1960, a child of nine was playing with her friends in a park in Southampton. No adults were around to supervise their play or even keep an eye on them. Later that day, the little girl's hideously mutilated body was found in undergrowth; she had been stabbed thirty-eight times. The killer was one of the children present in the park that day. Eight years later, in 1968, a little boy popped into the corner shop near his home in the northern English city of Newcastle. After leaving the shop alone, he was abducted and murdered by a 10-year-old girl.

There are a number of points to think about here. First, it is not being suggested that murders of the sort we have just looked at were very common in the 1960s, merely that they happened and that unaccompanied children, out and about in public places, faced a definite risk of death. In other words, some of them would not have their 'common sense' increased or be given the opportunity to grow up to be 'better adults' by these experiences; instead, visits to the park, popping to the local corner shop and walking to school alone were, quite literally, the death of them. This is sometimes forgotten when discussing childhood at that time. Those who claim that children today should be able to play in the park and visit the corner shop alone are presumably saying that a certain number of avoidable deaths are a reasonable price to pay for such increased freedom on the part of those who will not be murdered or knocked down and killed by cars. Obviously, the three deaths at which we have just looked would not have happened if the children had not been out by themselves, but were rather accompanied by their parents or other responsible adults, as many of us now feel is desirable and wise.

Secondly, it was not only the danger of sudden death which was faced by children playing out in the streets and parks without adults. In 1975 Cynthia Illingworth, a doctor in Sheffield, published a paper which analysed injuries to children using playground equipment such as swings, roundabouts and slides. This was at a time when it was common practice for parents to send an older child to the park in charge of younger siblings. One might perhaps have a boy of 10 or 11 sent to the park with his five-year-old sister. This again is part of the golden age about which so many baby boomers now feel nostalgic. Dr Illingworth found that thousands of small children were suffering fractured skulls, broken arms and various other serious injuries; some were even being killed. Staff at the casualty departments at hospitals to whom she spoke likened the injuries seen from such accidents to those encountered in road-accident victims. Many of these children had been playing in parks, usually without their parents. One of the chief causes of such injuries was that, to quote the report which Dr Illingworth later produced, 'The younger children were at particular risk on equipment such as the wooden rocking horse or roundabout, when the speed of operation could be controlled by older children.' Yet one more disadvantage of leaving children in the park to play by themselves! We shall explore the dangers of playgrounds and parks in detail in Chapter 5. Illustration 3 shows a British playground in the 1950s. In this photograph, adults are present, which ameliorated some of the hazard for smaller children. Illustration 4 is of the kind of rocking horse about which Cynthia Illingworth wrote. It will be very familiar to older readers, some of whom might remember their own mishaps while playing on this iconic piece of playground equipment.

Another random statistic: in the 1950s, 300 children a year in Britain permanently lost the sight in one eye. This blindness resulted almost entirely from assaults by other children, using catapults, bows and arrows, airguns, stones, fireworks and bottles. Today, a single child being blinded in this way is likely to be reported in the press. These injuries were almost invariably inflicted when adults were not around to intervene when things were getting out of hand. The 3,000 British children who were blinded in one eye in this way during the 1950s are presumably to be regarded as yet more collateral damage. It seems a heavy price to pay, so that the other children who had not lost an eye while 'playing out' could grow up to be better adults and have their common sense increased.

The book by Steve Stack, a quotation from which we examined above, is by no means exceptional. Precisely the same sentiments are to be found in many other books, newspapers, magazines, television programmes, Internet discussions and personal conversations with those who recall the baby boomer years fondly. All tend to illustrate the difficulties in finding out what the past was really like. There is no doubt that the middle-aged and elderly men and women expressing these view are perfectly honest and telling the truth as they understand it, but this does not necessarily mean that they are right. It is, for instance possible genuinely to think that the fruit which one ate as a child was sweeter and tasted better, even though the true explanation has more to do with the declining number of taste buds in mature years. The same might well apply to memories of eternally sunny summer holidays and snowy Christmases. Memory can be an unreliable thing. For this reason, we must delve a little deeper than merely listening to and recording the subjective impressions of people who were children at the time.

This is not a trivial matter of disputing the recollections of this or that pensioner. Collectively, the reminiscences of the baby boomers have somehow ended up being treated as clinical data upon which government policy should be founded. The wholly erroneous belief that the streets of fifty or sixty years ago were free of what we now call 'feral' youths has led to laws being passed which forbid young people even to walk along certain designated streets. The idea of the so-called 'obesity epidemic' leads to a 'sugar tax'; worries about an apparent lack of exercise by children has resulted in an official policy to encourage school pupils to walk to school; misleading ideas about a rise in illiteracy causes governments to champion educational techniques which are said to have been successful in the 1950s, although there is no real evidence that this was so. In short, the supposed superiority of childhood during the formative years of the baby boomers over modern childhood has become an official doctrine which is shaping our society.

Other than the fanciful and distorted tales which older people traditionally tell of their childhood days, what reason do we have to believe that childhood in the 1950s or 1960s really was better in any way than today? Moving beyond just anecdotal evidence, which for one reason and another may not be wholly reliable, takes us into deep waters. On the face of it, nothing could be simpler. Why not just analyse the facts and figures from the years following the end of the Second World War and then compare them with what is happening now? Surely in that way, we will be able to build up a detailed and objective picture of the two periods and see just how they shape up against each other? Unfortunately, this is quite impossible.

There are several difficulties with just listing various statistics relating to 1957 or 1967 and then comparing them with similar data for 2017 and hoping to be able to see how things have changed over the last sixty years. Sometimes the information is not available and even when it is, the methods used for measuring various things about the condition and achievements of children have changed completely. A few examples will make this clearer. Let us consider first a claim frequently made in the press; that the academic attainments of children today are inferior to those of fifty or sixty years ago. This is often described in terms of the 'dumbing down' of our educational system. One aspect of this is that illiteracy is said to be on the rise and indeed to be approaching epidemic proportions. It is often suggested in newspapers, using official figures, that one British adult in five is functionally illiterate; a far higher rate than was believed to exist in the 1950s or 1960s. Surely, this figure alone tells us that something is seriously wrong with modern schools? Why can't we go back to the old ways of teaching, which reduced illiteracy to practically zero? It is this perception which led several years ago to the officially recommended adoption in most maintained state schools of the use of phonics for teaching children to read. Out went all the trendy, whole-word teaching methods popular in the 1970s, along with the 'real books' schemes of the 1980s and instead, the sounds of the alphabet were once again emphasized.

Appearances are proverbially deceptive and this is very definitely the case with the apparently declining levels of literacy in this country caused, according to some, by sloppy teaching and by others the widespread use of mobile telephones and other digital technology. Until the 1970s, there was a very simple, rough-and-ready means of determining whether or not an individual was literate. Literacy was defined as the ability to read and write a simple note. If one could write, 'Gone to shops, Back in ten minutes' or read such a communication from another person, then you were literate. These days, more precise and, it is claimed, scientific methods are used and simply being able to read and write is not considered enough to be described as 'literate'. People are tested on, among other things, their so-called 'document literacy'. This is based upon the ability to decipher bus timetables and other tables and charts. There have always been plenty of people who struggle to work out when the next bus is due, the author of this book being one of them! It is this group, those who cannot always extract information from charts and tables or make sense of newspaper articles from the *Guardian*, who are now officially regarded as illiterate. In short, literacy is defined by the ability to gain a GCSE in English Language of at least Grade C. Using the same method of measurement as that used in the 1950s would reveal that the actual literacy rate in today's Britain is, just as it was then, virtually 100 per cent.

Much the same thing happens when we try to work out whether or not children in the 1950s were really leaner and healthier than those at school today. Some readers may be aware of the dramatic rise in obesity which struck the world in 1998, when the Body Mass Index threshold used to calculate whether a person was overweight was arbitrarily reduced from 27 to 25. Overnight, twenty-nine million Americans became overweight or obese. In this country, an 'obesity time bomb' was created, with many hundreds of thousands of people, including children, being classified as overweight. When the goalposts are being shifted in this way, it becomes very difficult to know if we are comparing like with like.

As with literacy and obesity, so too with crime and anti-social behaviour. Take knife and gun crime, for instance. As I write, newspapers are full of alarming headlines which talk of a rise in gun crime, with children as young as 10 being arrested for firearms-related offences. At first sight, this all sounds quite horrifying. Surely we cannot deny that this is a new trend? Children weren't toting guns in the 1950s, were they? Except of course, they were. Close reading of the articles beneath these terrifying headlines reveal that by 'firearms offences', the police are lumping together the figures relating not only to actual firearms, but also starting pistols, air rifles and replica weapons. If we rephrase the question as, 'Were 10 and 11-year-olds in the 1950s playing around with airguns?', then the answer is of course that they were; far more than is the case today. The *Just William* stories often mention William's affection for airguns and in real life, air pistols and air rifles were all over the place. Boys' comics carried advertisements for airguns and these were taken out to play with an alarming frequency. Illustration 5 shows an unremarkable advertisement from 1957, designed to persuade fathers to give their 10- and 11-year-old sons air rifles for birthday or Christmas presents. In those days, of course, no policeman would have dreamed of arresting a boy with an airgun. If the thing was obviously being misused, then he might step in and take the boy home, giving a few words of advice to the parents, but other than that airguns were accepted as a fact of life.

A similar situation exists with knives and knife crime. If a police officer sixty years ago saw a 12-year-old with a knife, then he would not even have bothered to break his step. After all, practically all boys carried knives at that time. We are far less tolerant today of children and teenagers carrying around potentially deadly weapons and so arrests and convictions for the possession of knives and guns have soared. This tells us very little and certainly does not tend to suggest an 'epidemic' of knife or gun crime. Illustration 6 shows an open penknife of the kind carried by almost every baby boomer boy at some time or another.

All of which makes it extraordinarily difficult to obtain a rounded picture of childhood and adolescence in the decades following the end of the Second World War, one that may profitably be compared with the situation today. Nevertheless, the attempt will be made, drawing upon newspaper reports, contemporary observations and what records do exist. The result might be more than a little surprising to anybody who has formed a view on the childhood experiences of the baby boomers relying only on their own recollections in late middle age, or what is worse, from reading what is said about this era in newspapers and magazines.

Chapter 1

The Land of Lost Content:
Childhood in the Good Old Days

For most of recorded history, older people have been in the habit of claiming that everything was a good deal better during their own childhoods than is now the case. The summers were longer, the fruit sweeter, the food more wholesome and the world an altogether happier and less complicated place when they were young. Not only that, but the children themselves were different in the old days. They were more obedient, industrious, well-behaved, polite, happy and healthy. Such sentiments were being expressed centuries before the birth of Christ and the notion is still going strong; that this modern world is not a patch on the one which existed fifty or sixty years ago and children not what they once were. The Old Testament book of Ecclesiastes was composed in the third century BC, perhaps 2,300 years ago. Its author wrote, 'Never ask, "Oh, why were thing so much better in the old days?" It's not an intelligent question.'

This imaginary world, very different from our own and the children much happier, has always lingered tantalisingly on the edge of living memory, so close that we feel that our generation has only just missed it. It is generally the time in which our parents or grandparents grew up. In the last century of so, the golden age was the Edwardian Era before the First World War and then later, the years before the outbreak of the Second World War in 1939. Today, it is the 1950s and 1960s which were such a wonderful time to be young. Children at that time had, according to some of those who were children in those days, unlimited freedom to roam a world which was safe and inviting; a strange and magical land where no serious harm ever befell children, as long as they made sure to be home by teatime.

A. E. Housman summed up perfectly this yearning for a vanished, enchanted world, when he wrote:

Into my heart an air that kills

From yon far country blows:
What are those blue remembered hills,
What spires, what farms are those?

That is the land of lost content,
I see it shining plain,
The happy highways where I went
And cannot come again.

Most of us, at least when we are young, tend to take this sort of thing with a pinch of salt. When Granny tells us how much healthier everybody was in the old days, with all the fresh air and exercise that they got, and the food eaten wasn't contaminated with all those dreadful additives and other chemicals, we listen politely but without placing too much credence upon her tales. Similarly, when we are informed that children in the past were better behaved, stronger, healthier, happier, more polite, pluckier, possessed of greater reserves of initiative and studied harder at school or that the summers were longer and the winters snowier, we treat these assertions with caution. After all, memory can be faulty and there is no reason at all to suppose that recollections of this sort from over half a century ago are wholly accurate and objective. It is hardly likely that the world really *was* a better place when our parents and grandparents were little children, nor that children were really all that different, whatever we might now be told.

There are a number of factors at work when we see older people constructing fantasy worlds of this sort; some physiological, others psychological. Beginning first with the way in which physiological deterioration as we grow older helps shapes our memories of childhood, it must be borne in mind that once we pass our mid-twenties, our faculties and senses usually begin to decline and fail. We have fewer taste buds and those we do have shrink and are less efficient. The range of sounds we are able to detect shrinks; our eyesight is seldom as keen in later years as it was in our youth. All of which means that our earliest memories of tastes, for instance, will seem more vivid and rich than those we actually experience in middle and old age. Few of us wish to confront our own failing faculties and declining vitality and it is therefore more reassuring and satisfying to pretend that the fault lies with modern food, rather than our own bodies. It's not that our tongues are gradually becoming less sensitive, the blame lies rather with this awful stuff that the shops sell now. When we were children, you could buy apples which *tasted* like apples. Everything today is so tasteless and bland!

Another reason why childhood experiences are remembered as being richer and more enjoyable than those in middle or old age is psychological, rather than physiological. The *first* time we encounter something, whether it is eating an ice cream or walking through snow, will always make more of an impression upon us than the hundreds or thousands of subsequent times we go through the experience. There is the exhilarating sense of novelty about early childhood experiences which cause them to stand out as being particularly vivid and memorable. From swimming in a river for the first time to sliding down a hill on a toboggan, the first time is always likely to be recalled in the future as the best of all. This is another of the factors at work when older people claim that their childhoods were marvellous, far more exciting than the way things are now. For them, this is perfectly true, but it tells us little about the objective state of the world, either then or now.

Human memory is not a passive process of simply pointing our eyes and ears at a scene and recording faithfully all that is seen and heard. It consists rather of an active and continuous mechanism of editing and enhancing the original sense impressions, discarding some and enlarging others. Why would we wish to retain memories of disappointment and sadness when we were little, in preference to images of pleasure and enjoyment? This too contributes to our skewed perspective when looking back at our schooldays from the perspective of fifty years or so of subsequent life. How else are we to explain why so many older people recall the past with such enthusiasm, claiming that their schooldays were the happiest of their lives? It is curious, and more than a little suspicious, that one never meets a 14-year-old who believes this to be true.

It is often expressly stated that fewer children were being abducted or murdered by strangers during the 1950s and that children were able to play freely out of doors without the risk of falling prey to predatory paedophiles. This is quite untrue, as a quick trawl through newspaper archives soon reveals. The reason for this particular misconception is not hard to find. These days, news of a murder will spread around the Internet before it even reaches the newspapers. It would be all but impossible to prevent a child with a mobile telephone from finding out about all sorts of horrors, including child abuse and murder. This was not the case fifty or sixty years ago. Few children at that time were avid newspaper readers and if they didn't listen to the news on the radio or watch it on television then they would be most unlikely to hear about murders involving children.

There is a natural, widespread and understandable tendency for parents to shield and protect their children from unpalatable or distasteful aspects of life, in case they become distressed or frightened about the terrible things which have befallen some child of similar age to them. For this reason, and because it was easily accomplished in the pre-electronic media years of the baby boomers' childhoods, there was a tacit conspiracy among adults to conceal news of dreadful murders or child abuse. It was felt that there was no need to draw attention to such things in any case, having a bearing as they sometimes did upon sexual depravity, sexual activity of any kind being a taboo subject for discussion in most families at that time. It is for this reason that many baby boomers did not realize then, and have never taken the trouble in later years to find out, about the child murders and sexual abuse of children at the time that they were growing up. One or two especially dreadful cases might have filtered through to them, the so-called Moors Murderers being one of these, but in general child abuse or murders were unknown to children at that time.

The baby boomers are merely the latest generation to wax wistful about their wonderful childhoods. The term 'baby boomer' itself might perhaps need a little explanation. During the Second World War, with many husbands away fighting, the birth rate, for obvious reasons, dropped. At the end of the war in 1945, the large-scale resumption of connubial activity resulting from the return of the servicemen who had been away from home led to a surge in births nine months later. This rise in the birth rate lasted for nearly twenty years and became known facetiously as the post-war 'baby boom'. Children born between roughly 1946 and 1964 are therefore popularly known as baby boomers.

The baby boomers, who now range in age from their early fifties to perhaps 70 years of age, enthusiastically promote the idea that the past was a glorious place, particularly for children, who were of course all happier and healthier than kids today as well as enjoying far more freedom. So far, so good, and in proclaiming their affection for a lost world of childhood where everything was better than it is now, the baby boomers are doing no more than their parents and grandparents had done before them. Here is a piece which sums up this view of childhood during the thirty years or so which followed the end of the Second World War. It is worth quoting this account, which in various forms has been circulating for several years on the Internet, at length, for it contains a number of themes at which we shall later be looking in detail. In 2012, the *Daily Mail* described this as 'the new online sensation'. The newspaper went on to say that it was, 'A lyrical evocation of growing up in the Forties, Fifties and Sixties, when children were safe to play where they liked'. Again, we note the curious idea that children were safe when they played out of doors sixty years ago, in a way that is no longer the case. By implication, the streets and fields of Britain have become more dangerous with the passage of time.

CONGRATULATIONS TO ALL WHO WERE BORN IN THE 1940's, 50's, 60's! First, we survived being born to mothers who smoked and/or drank while they carried us and lived in houses made of asbestos. They took aspirin, ate blue cheese, raw egg products, loads of bacon and processed meat, tuna from a can, and didn't get tested for diabetes or cancer. Then after that trauma, our baby cots were covered with bright coloured lead-based paints. We had no childproof lids on medicine bottles, doors or cabinets and when we rode our bikes, we had no helmets or shoes, not to mention the risks we took hitchhiking. As children, we would ride in cars with no seat belts or air bags.

Take away food was limited to fish and chips, no pizza shops, McDonalds, KFC or Subway. Even though all the shops closed at 6.00pm and didn't open on the weekends, somehow we didn't starve to death! We ate cupcakes, white bread and real butter and drank soft drinks with sugar in it, but we weren't overweight because . . . WE WERE ALWAYS OUTSIDE PLAYING!!

We would leave home in the morning and play all day, as long as we were back by teatime. No one was able to reach us all day. And we were O.K. We built tree houses and dens and played in river beds with Matchbox cars. We did not have Playstations, Nintendo Wii, X-boxes, no video games at all, no 999 TV channels, no video/dvd films, no mobile phones, no personal computers, no Internet or Internet chat rooms . . . WE HAD FRIENDS and we went outside and found them! We fell out of trees, got cut, broke bones and teeth and there were no lawsuits from these accidents. You could buy Easter Eggs and Hot Cross Buns only at Easter time. We were given air guns and catapults for our tenth birthdays and rode bikes to our friends' houses.

Our teachers used to hit us with canes and gym shoes and bullies always ruled the playground at school. We had freedom, failure, success and responsibility, and we learned HOW TO DEAL WITH IT ALL!

And YOU are one of them! CONGRATULATIONS! You might want to share this with others who have had the luck to grow up as kids, before the lawyers and the government regulated our lives for our own good. And while you are at it, forward it to your kids so they will know how brave their parents were!

We note that the children born in the post-war years were apparently in the habit of leaving their homes in the morning, at weekends and during school holidays, spending all day in the streets or fields and only returning for their tea. This particular claim has become something of a *leit motif* for baby boomers; it regularly crops up whenever discussion turns to the difference between childhood in those days and the situation now. Here is Robert Elms, the writer and broadcaster, describing his own childhood in the 1960s: 'By the time I was nine or ten it became a ritual to be given the money for a one-day bus pass known as a Red Rover and the instruction to come back in time for tea.' The memory of playing out all day, without the presence of any adults, from breakfast until teatime is a powerful one for many adults born between 1946 and 1964. It invariably crops up when they are talking about their childhood. Going out by themselves to play and walking to and from school without their parents, has come to be seen as a desirable way of life, one denied to modern children, with dreadful consequences such as the likelihood of developing life-limiting diseases in later life.

It is very right and proper that older people should believe that their own childhoods were richer, more stimulating and generally an improvement on the lives lived by modern children and if they wish to pretend that their lives as children were like one long Enid Blyton adventure, then this does not hurt anybody. It is a harmless-enough piece of make-believe. In recent years though, rather than merely listening indulgently to these stories, we are increasingly being expected to treat the fanciful reminiscences of men and women in their sixties and seventies as being reliable data, upon which we should act, or even use to formulate government policy. Books are being published with titles such as *Toxic Childhood*, which purport to show that modern children really *are* worse off in many ways than their older relatives were at a similar age, suffering from mental health problems, physical ailments, restricted liberty and various other awful consequences of being born into this modern world. Even more bizarrely, government agencies and health trusts are now writing policies, and even framing legislation, which seemingly acknowledge that childhood today is somehow failing and in need of rescuing to make it more like the way of life enjoyed by children in the 1950s. All of which is a little disconcerting, to say the least of it! This peculiar trend is best illustrated by looking first at one of the most popular manifestations of this trend, the idea that today's children do not get enough exercise and that if we could only recreate the conditions under which children grew up during the 1950s and 1960s, then we would see a tremendous and beneficial change in the physical and mental health of British children. This is thought to be a good idea for several reasons, not least of which is that such a radical change of lifestyle is necessary to tackle what is sometimes called the 'obesity epidemic' or 'obesity time bomb'. All such ideas are predicated on the assumption that children in previous generations were healthier and fitter than young people today and that the best way to improve the health of the rising generation is to take steps to replicate the experience of the baby boomers.

In 2014 the British government published a draft Cycling Delivery Plan, designed to increase the number of people who travel on bicycle and by foot. One of the targets was that within the next ten years, the percentage of children aged between five and ten who walk to school should rise to 55 per cent. A laudable enough aim, one might think and just the sort of thing to get children to exercise more. Surely, a return to the days when children walked to school, rather than being driven by their parents, could only be a good target to strive for? After all, forty years ago, the overwhelming majority of children *did* walk to school and were in consequence much fitter and healthier than today's youngsters. This, at least, is the received view.

There can be no doubt at all that children in the first three decades after the end of the Second World War spent far more time out and about in the streets without adults. This included playing with their friends after school and at weekends, as well as walking to and from school. In 1971, for example, over 80 per cent of seven- and eight-year-olds walked to school alone. Twenty years later, this figure had fallen below 10 per cent and today it would be surprising to see any seven-year-old arrive regularly at school having walked there alone. Indeed, so unusual would this be that it would almost certainly be the object of unfavourable remark by other parents and probably teachers as well. If a child of that age continued to arrive at school unaccompanied by an adult, then it is entirely possible that Social Services would be notified. At which point, many baby boomers will begin muttering things like 'The Nanny State!' and 'Health and Safety gone mad!' Surely it makes sense that children should be given the chance to become independent without a lot of mollycoddling and fuss? After all, the baby boomers themselves didn't come to any harm did they? Why *shouldn't* today's children be accorded a similar amount of freedom to that which was enjoyed fifty years ago? It definitely made for a more healthy lifestyle, didn't it?

The description of baby boomer childhood from the Internet, which we saw above, contains this claim 'we weren't overweight because . . . WE WERE ALWAYS OUTSIDE PLAYING!! We would leave home in the morning and play all day, as long as we were back by teatime. No one was able to reach us all day. And we were O.K.'

'We were O.K.' How true actually is this statement? If we wish to know what childhood was like in the 1950s and 1960s, we shall sometimes have to look at records and statistics from that time and use those as the basis for our investigations, combining them where necessary with newspaper reports and other contemporaneous accounts. This is the method used in this book and using such sources to examine the hazards to health faced by the baby boomers reveals a number of shocking facts, facts which nobody seems anxious to acknowledge today. Looking at the genuine situation of the baby boomer children shows just how healthy and safe, or otherwise, their lives actually were.

As a woman remarks sadly on the Netmums site, regretting the restricted circumstances of her own child's experiences: 'I miss the carefree childhood. I could play out from 8 am to 6 pm and my Mum never had to worry I would be snatched.' This is an interesting idea. Were children safer from being 'snatched' a few decades ago? It was not of course only seven- and eight-year-olds who walked to school alone in those days; even six-year-olds were sent off by their mothers every morning to make their own way to school and back. On 8 September 1965, six-year-old Margaret Reynolds set off alone for school. She lived in the Aston district of Birmingham. Little Margaret didn't arrive at school that day and nothing more was heard of her for four months. Five-year-olds too were allowed to travel the streets on their own back in 1965. On 30 December that year, five-year-old Diana Tift was walking to her grandmother's house in Bloxwich, when she too simply vanished. The following month the corpses of the missing little girls were found lying side by side in a ditch. They had been murdered.

This then is one of those things that happened during the childhood years of the baby boomers about which we seldom hear. Obviously, little girls of five and six are far more likely to be abducted if they are walking the streets alone than when they are accompanied by their parents. Still, it may be argued, such murders must surely have been freakishly rare? This is true, although we might ask ourselves how often a wandering maniac would be likely to encounter a little girl whom he could snatch off the streets today. It is hard to recall when last a child of five was kidnapped and killed in this way in Britain by a random stranger; there simply aren't that many opportunities for such crimes these days.

If the murder of a child by a complete stranger is today a very unusual occurrence, so too is being killed crossing the road. In an average year in this country, only about twenty young people under the age of 16 are knocked down and killed by cars. Of course, as any baby boomer will tell you, there were far fewer cars about during their childhood, which must have made the streets safer for them, or so we are supposed to believe. In 1965, the same year that Margaret Reynolds and Diana Tift were

murdered, over 900 child pedestrians were killed by traffic in Britain
Somewhere in the region of forty-five times as many children died
crossing the road that year as are likely to be killed by cars this year. It
can hardly be doubted that this was mainly due to the fact that so many
young children were out and about, crossing roads by themselves. This
was part of the human cost of the baby boomers walking to school alone
and playing out until teatime. In fact, the raw data for traffic accidents are
a little misleading; the situation was even worse than at first appears. There
were only a third as many cars on the roads fifty years ago. This means
that a car in 1965 was 135 times as likely to knock down and kill a child
as a car today. A sobering thought indeed and one which causes us to raise
our eyebrows at the idea that it will improve the health of modern children
if they are encouraged to walk to school, rather than travelling in cars. If
children started playing out all day and walking to school by themselves
the first thing we would see, before any fall in obesity levels, would be
soaring statistics for deaths and serious injuries among child pedestrians
Despite this, there is a concerted effort throughout Britain to try and get
more children to walk to school, because this kept children fit and healthy
in the 1950s and 1960s.

The results of such official nostalgia for 1960s childhood may be seen
in Wales. In 2009, the Welsh Assembly government launched a walking
and cycling initiative, a flagship policy to get more adults walking and
cycling to work, along with children using these methods to travel to
school. The following year, the number of children walking to school had
risen and this was hailed as a triumph in the battle against obesity. Four
years later, those collating statistics for child casualties on the roads
noticed a disturbing trend. For two years running, in 2013 and 2014, a rise
in the number of child pedestrians being seriously injured on the roads
was noted. In 2014, there was a 12 per cent increase in children under 16
suffering serious injuries. For a policy designed to improve health by
reducing obesity, this was a regrettable side-effect.

The baby boomer years were not really safer and more healthy for
children in any respect, on the roads or elsewhere. In 1970, deaths from
accidental causes for children were running at 17.5 per 100,000 in
England. Thirty years later, this had dropped to 4.5 per 100,000; it is now
about 2.7 per 100,000. In other words, about seven times as many children

were being killed accidentally in the 1960s as are now. Compared with
the years when the first baby boomers were born, the situation is even
more striking. Ten times as many children were being killed in accidents
in the mid-1940s compared with today. When baby boomers complain, as
regularly happens, about Health and Safety, they do tend to forget how
many children's lives are being saved by it.

What of the health generally of children of the baby boomer generation?
It has to be said that the picture is consistently and unremittingly grim.
Looking back at the document taken from the Internet, we see that: 'First,
we survived being born to mothers who smoked and/or drank while they
carried us and lived in houses made of asbestos. They took aspirin, ate
blue cheese, raw egg products, loads of bacon and processed meat, tuna
from a can, and didn't get tested for diabetes or cancer.' Again, this sums
up the point of view of an awful lot of baby boomers. These things didn't
do them any harm, so why all the fuss now? Of course, the adults today
who were born during that period certainly did survive; that much is
indisputable. What though of the babies and children who did not? We
seldom hear about them. The statement, 'we survived being born to
mothers who . . .' is, to say the least of it, misleading. The infant mortality
rate in 1960, the proportion of babies who died before their first birthday,
was five times what it is today. The percentage of babies who died in
infancy in Britain that year is roughly the same as a modern-day Third-
World country such as Egypt. Nor was the situation very good for older
children.

Most of the great killer diseases in modern Britain, things such as cancer
and heart disease, tend to strike almost exclusively at adults. The death of
a child under 16 from illness is a terrible, but thankfully rare, occurrence.
These days, we view the death of even a single child from an infectious
disease as being a shocking tragedy and if two or three die in an outbreak
of disease, we are alarmed and demand answers from the medical
authorities. For the baby boomers though, the death of children from
illness, especially infectious diseases, was routine. In 1947, the year after
the birth of the first baby boomers, an epidemic of polio swept Britain.
There were 8,000 cases that year, resulting in the death of many children
and the crippling of a very large number of those who survived the illness.
As late as 1960, there were eighty deaths in Britain from polio and many

children left with varying degrees of disability, ranging from slight limp to being permanently confined to wheelchairs. In that same year, there were 750,000 cases of measles, leading to the deaths of 150 children. A much larger number were left deaf or with brain damage.

Younger readers might not be aware of the dreadful epidemics which swept the country with monotonous regularity during the 1940s and 1950s. Measles, polio, whooping cough, scarlet fever, diphtheria, German measles and mumps: all these killed children and left others crippled, sterile, deaf, blind or with irreversible brain damage. In 1953, there were 46,546 cases of tuberculosis in Britain, which resulted in over 8,000 deaths. Even smallpox was still a hazard for the baby boomers. These random figures might give some idea of the risks faced by children at that time. Often, such infectious diseases struck hardest against young children who were far more likely to die of them than were healthy adults. Sometimes environmental disasters struck the country, hitting babies and children the hardest. In December 1952 came London's Great Smog which killed over 5,000 people. During that winter, the infant mortality rate in the capital doubled.

The more closely we examine the 'land of lost content' in which the baby boomers grew to adulthood, the less appetising it appears! Almost a thousand children a year being knocked down and killed by traffic, child murders, epidemics of infectious diseases which killed hundreds and left thousands crippled for life, rampant knife and gun crime, unchecked sexual abuse: these are just a few of the hazards facing children born between 1946 and 1964. Far from being golden age of childhood, as is sometimes claimed, it was a dangerous time for children to be alive.

We saw that the yearning for a vanished and happier world for children has been around for many years, but the current obsession with the childhood of half a century or more ago does seem to be qualitatively different in some ways from the general and traditional feelings about childhood in the past. When a country's politicians and professionals work together to try and recreate some kind of facsimile of the past, enacting legislation and imposing policies upon hospitals, schools and the general public in the process, then there is clearly something a little strange going on. Successive governments, along with countless older people. and even those who weren't even born until a couple of decades after the baby boomers, all seem convinced that opportunities for a joyously happy and fulfilling childhood somehow came to an end round about 1980, at the time when the last baby boomers, those born in 1964, were leaving school. This is exceedingly odd.

1980 is of course significant for more than the fact that it marked childhood's end for the baby boomers. It was also the time that computers, electronic games, compact discs, videos and a host of other things which were to make the world such a different place began to be seen in Britain. In short, it signalled the onset of what one might call the electronic era and the beginning of the digital revolution. This digital revolution is still in full swing and it has had every bit as great an impact on life in this country as the Industrial Revolution did in the late eighteenth and early nineteenth centuries. Not everybody in Victorian Britain was wildly enthusiastic about the visible manifestations of the Industrial Revolution, such things as factory chimneys belching smoke, noisy railway trains, the rapid growth of urban slums, the increasingly frantic speed with which people could communicate by telegraph and so on. They yearned for a gentler, pre-industrial world, with finer values than those they saw in the present day. Such people turned to the Middle Ages for their inspiration, a time when chivalry, stability and old-fashioned values were still, or so it was claimed, to be found in the world. This mania for the medieval period spawned the revival of Gothic architecture, the art of the Pre-Raphaelite Brotherhood, poetry such as Tennyson's *Idylls of the King* and William Morris and the Arts and Craft Movement. Even Queen Victoria became a fan of medievalism, she and her husband posing for statues and paintings showing them as historical figures from the era such as Edward III and Queen Philippa.

The craze for the medieval was essentially a rejection of the modern world of mid-Victorian Britain, especially the ugliness of industry, and a desire to embrace a more attractive-looking past. Something very similar appears to be happening today with what looks rather like a longing for a pre-*digital* past. Whenever twenty-first-century childhood is under discussion by baby boomers, it seems to be the digital technology with which children are so familiar which excites the greatest unease. Somebody will be sure to mention that when he or she was at school, they had to use long division and there were no calculators to help them.

Somebody else will observe that it's all computers today and that children and teenagers now spend their whole time talking on mobiles or connected to the Internet, with all its attendant perils. To listen to some politicians too, one gets the impression that most of the problems faced by today's children are somehow bound up with digital technology. The various screens are making them lazy and causing them to become overweight and develop diabetes, the calculators on their phones are harming their ability to do sums, textspeak is damaging their literacy skills, the Internet is making them obsessed with violence and sex: everything seems to be mixed up with digital devices of one sort or another. We will look more at this idea later on.

This chapter has provided an overview of the themes at which we shall be looking. In the wake of the revelations about endemic sexual abuse of children in the 1960s and 1970s by celebrities, it might be a good idea to begin by looking at attitudes to underage children, especially girls, at the time the baby boomers were growing up. This will be of particular interest, because many people today are simply unable to understand how abuse on an industrial scale was carried out more or less in plain sight at that time. The answer lies rooted in Britain's past, which fashioned and shaped how many men saw young girls at that time. Readers should be warned in advance that some of this is exceedingly shocking to modern sensibilities.

Chapter 2

'Dumb But Pretty, Like a Schoolgirl Should Be':
The Sexual Abuse of Children in the Post-War Years

In recent years, we have heard a great deal about the sexual abuse of children which was being carried out in Britain during the 1960s and 1970s by well-known entertainers, television presenters and others. The obvious question is how it was possible for these men to get away with such activities for so long. During the high-profile investigations into the lives and careers of men such as Jimmy Savile, Rolf Harris and Stuart Hall, a phrase began to be widely used to describe the process by which wholesale abuse of this sort could take place without anybody apparently noticing what was going on. It was called 'hiding in plain sight'. So commonly did the expression crop up in this connection that when a biography of the disc jockey Jimmy Savile was published in 2015, it bore the title *In Plain Sight*.

To see how the sexual abuse of children in the period at which we are looking could be undertaken 'in plain sight', it will be necessary to look back considerably further than just the seventy years or so which separate us from the birth of the first baby boomers. Before doing so, we will examine a film made at the end of the 1960s, one which sheds light on the *mores* of British society at that time, particularly as they relate to sexual activity with very young girls. Only by looking at material such as this will it be possible to understand the attitudes which were prevalent when the baby boomers were growing up and so understand why it was that the indecent assault and even rape of young girls was at that time viewed with far more tolerance than is now the case. Prevailing standards of behaviour then, regarding girls under the legal age of consent, contrast very greatly with what is now considered acceptable.

In 1969 a mainstream British film called *Lola* was produced. It had what might justly be called an all-star cast. Among those who appeared in the film were Honor Blackman, Jimmy Tarbuck, Charles Bronson, Susan

George, Jack Hawkins, Robert Morley and Lionel Jeffries. Even Trevor
Howard, famous for his starring role in *Brief Encounter*, was in it. The
film was directed by Richard Donner, who went on to direct *Superman*
and *Lethal Weapon*. Originally, the film was called *Twinky* and it is from
the title song, of the same name, that the quotation at the beginning of this
chapter comes. 'Dumb but pretty, like a schoolgirl should be' sounds more
than a little sleazy and suspect to modern ears; as well it might!

Some idea of the plot of *Lola* may be gleaned by simply looking at one
of the posters which advertised it. It shows a schoolgirl in uniform and
wearing white knee socks, together with a harassed-looking middle-aged
man. The captions read; 'She's almost 16', 'He's almost 40' and 'It may
be love . . . but it's definitely exhausting!' This film is about a middle-
aged pornographer's sexual relationship with, and subsequent marriage
to, a schoolgirl. It is supposedly a romantic comedy and not one of those
who produced, directed or acted in it, apparently saw anything in the least
distasteful about the subject matter. The title of the film, incidentally, is a
conscious reference to that most famous exploration of the mind of a
predatory paedophile; Vladimir Nabokov's *Lolita*! The central character
in the film, played by Charles Bronson, alludes to *Lolita*, when he admits
to being a nymphetishist and calls his schoolgirl lover 'Lola' in tribute to
this inspiration.

The song at the beginning of *Lola*, written and sung by Jim Dale, reveals
that the eponymous heroine is not in fact 'almost 16', but just a little past
her sixteenth birthday. Jim Dale also wrote the lyrics of the song Georgie
Girl, which was a hit for The Seekers and became something of an anthem
of the Swinging Sixties, following its release in 1966. The opening words
of the title song of *Lola* or *Twinky* are:

Never met a girl like this for me,
Dumb but pretty like a schoolgirl should be,

It continues, by telling us that the subject of the man's affections is:

Sixteen summers and a month or two,
A grown-up lover when the girls can't see you.

These couplets are sufficient to give the flavour of the thing. The singer goes on to compare the schoolgirl to Tinkerbell and say, 'When we touch, I feel like Peter Pan'. She is also referred to as 'Jezebel' and a 'Devil'.

The film at which we have just looked shows us exactly what was 'hiding in plain sight' for young girls of the baby boomer generation. It was not so much this or that singer or celebrity, but rather an entire mindset; one which accepted that schoolgirls were a legitimate object of sexual desire for grown men. That a film like *Lola* should excite amusement, rather than disgust, tells us a great deal about the way that children, particularly girls, were seen in those days.

Another illustration of how it was felt forty or fifty years ago to be quite acceptable for older men to express a sexual interest in young girls, often those below the age of legal consent, may be seen in a popular television programme made a few years after *Lola* was released. James Bolam and Rodney Bewes starred as the central characters of the situation comedy *Whatever Happened to the Likely Lads?*, which was broadcast in 1973 and 1974, at a time when they were in their late thirties. As with the film *Lola*, this was not the product of some sleazy Soho studio, but was rather one of the most popular sitcoms on television at that time. It was written by Dick Clement and Ian La Frenais, the people who gave us *Porridge*, *Lovejoy* and *Auf Wiedersehen Pet*. In the episode *Boys' Night In*, broadcast on 27 March 1973, Terry and Bob, played respectively by James Bolam and Rodney Bewes, talk about their favourite sexual fantasies. Terry says that, 'Sometimes, I'm the new master at a girls' high school.' Bob understands this perfectly, replying, 'Yes, gymslips. I've been worried about that. I think the sexiest TV programme is *Top of the Form*, not *Top of the Pops*.' The quiz programme *Top of the Form* featured teams of schoolchildren aged between 11 and 16. The fact that a man approaching 40 could describe the sight of underage girls as being sexy in this way and raise a laugh from the audience, tells us that there was something odd and disturbing going on in those days! It is this attitude, that girls of 11 and 12 upwards might be viewed as sexually attractive, which was at the root of much of the abuse which was endemic in the baby boomer years. Sometimes, as in the case of Jimmy Savile, this might mean indecent assault and rape. At other times, it entailed men exposing themselves to children, something which was horribly common in those days. All such offences had in common the fact that it was not regarded as all that reprehensible to lust after pubescent girls. Indeed, as we shall see, throughout almost the whole of the 1950s, it was not even a criminal offence to interfere with children, as long as one did it in a non-violent way! Before looking at this extraordinary state of affairs, which resulted from the Lord Chief Justice himself ruling in 1951 that no offence was being committed if a grown man persuaded a girl of nine to touch his penis, we must think a little about the overall mentality which allowed adults to fantasise about and abuse schoolgirls, often with complete impunity. The state of affairs, in fact, which allowed perverts like Jimmy Savile to prey freely upon children of the baby boomer generation.

It is sometimes forgotten that for most of the Victorian Era, the age of consent in Britain was 12. (Even this was an improvement on the situation at the beginning of the nineteenth century, when it was 10.) Girls of 12 and 13 married, had affairs and worked as prostitutes quite openly until the law was changed in 1875 and 1885, to raise the age of consent firstly to 13 and then to 16. That sexual activity with children was so common as to be unremarkable is neatly indicated by reading what the London correspondent of the French newspaper *Le Figaro* had to say of London in the early 1870s. He described how: 'Every evening towards midnight more than five hundred girls in ages between twelve and fifteen years parade between Piccadilly Circus and Waterloo Place, that is on a stretch of ground no more than three hundred yards long.' There was evidently no secret about the fact that children were openly prostituting themselves in the heart of London's West End.

Even more surprising is the fact that although the age of consent for sexual activity outside marriage was raised to 16 in 1885, it remained 12 for the purposes of marriage. It was not until the passing of the Age of Marriage Act in 1929 that it became unlawful to marry a 12-year-old girl. This has a bearing on how children that age were viewed in the past, attitudes which lingered on until the 1960s and 1970s. We looked at a film released at that time about a man who has a sexual affair with and eventually marries a schoolgirl. A notable aspect is that Susan George, as the girl, talks and acts in a very childish way, more like a 12-year-old than a young woman of 16. This too, the idea of the child-wife, and also the very young girl who acts and is treated as an adult, is an old British tradition.

The notion of schoolgirl as lover and prospective bride is a long-standing one in British literature. Such girls are to be found in the works of both Charles Dickens and Gilbert and Sullivan. In Dickens' *The Mystery of Edwin Drood*, the hero is engaged to be married to a schoolgirl. Rosa Budd, known inevitably as 'Rosebud', is of an indeterminate age; her behaviour though suggests a young child. She sucks her thumb, is eating an acid drop when her 'fiancé' comes to visit her at school and is generally portrayed as being immature and childish. Her chosen destination when taken out for the day is a sweet shop and after the visit, 'She remonstrates, laughing, and is a childish schoolgirl again.' Of course, the pages of Dicken's novels are littered with adult women who look like children, or girls who occupy the roles of adults. We think of Little Dorrit, who was so slight in stature and innocent in appearance that she was mistaken for a little girl, David Copperfield's child-wife Dora, Jenny Wren from *Our Mutual Friend* and many others. Ambivalent attitudes towards young girls in Dickens sometimes spill over into frankly paedophile descriptions, as when the villainous dwarf Quilp is pursuing Little Nell and her grandfather. Nell is a little girl, 'a small and delicate child of much sweetness of disposition', and yet Quilp desires her for his wife. Here he is, describing the child: 'Such a fresh, blooming, modest little bud . . . such a chubby, rosy, cosy little Nell . . . She's so small, so compact, so beautifully modelled . . . such little feet.' It is enough to make one's flesh creep!

It is not only our national author who features in his works young girls being pursued by adult males, often with no condemnation of their actions being implied. Perhaps Gilbert and Sullivan's best-loved operetta is *The Mikado*. In it, we meet another schoolgirl who is engaged to be married to one man and, like Rosa Budd, is the object of desire by somebody else as well. In this case, the girl is called Yum Yum; suggestive of a tasty morsel. Yum Yum, like Rosa Budd, is of an indeterminate age. She introduces herself and her sisters by singing with them:

Three little maids from school are we,
Pert as a school-girl well can be,
Filled to the brim with girlish glee
Three little maids from school.

These are not the only examples in Victorian literature of schoolgirls being presented as prospective sexual partners for grown man and a line may be drawn straight from this tradition, through the *St Trinian's* films to productions such as *Lola*, at which we looked above. What, some readers might be asking at this point, could possibly be wrong with the *St Trinian's* films? Surely, it was all harmless, British fun, with Alistair Sim cross-dressing as the hapless headmistress of the ill-fated school? There was in fact a distinctly dubious and unsavoury side to these films, produced during the baby boomer years, which in a way exemplified the problem at which we are looking in this chapter.

'Flash Harry', played by George Cole, in the *St Trinian's* films, ran the St Trinian's Matrimonial Agency, arranging dates with wealthy men for the schoolgirls. Once again, the idea that schoolgirl brides are somehow a desirable thing. In one of the films, a schoolgirl gets a job as a stripper. Some of the girls are played by actresses in their twenties, wearing absurdly skimpy gymslips, so short that their knickers are revealed. We are plainly meant to see them as attractive young women, rather than immature girls. It is this sexualisation of schoolgirls and acceptance of them as being appropriate targets for male attention which was hiding in plain sight in the 1960s and 1970s when people like Jimmy Savile were operating. Things have, mercifully, changed since then and a middle-aged man today who expressed an interest in having sex with or marrying a schoolgirl would be viewed askance, but at the time when the baby boomers were growing up, it was felt by many to be no more than a bit of saucy fun, at worst a little risqué, like a Donald McGill postcard.

This awful mindset, the openly-expressed belief that it was quite natural for adult men to find schoolgirls attractive or even to pursue them for sexual purposes, lingered on in this country until well into the 1980s and 1990s. It is still around of course, although not perhaps spoken of so casually and with the assumption that other men will sympathise with such a point of view in the way that we saw the characters in *Whatever Happened to the Likely Lads?* doing. As late as 1986 a major British film was produced, featuring a subplot involving sexual activity between a schoolgirl and a teacher presented in a light-hearted and supposedly amusing fashion. *Clockwise*, starring John Cleese, Penelope Wilton and Alison Steadman, was essentially a comedy road movie in which Cleese and a schoolgirl attempt to reach an important conference in time for him to give a speech. In the course of the journey, the girl reveals that she is having an affair with a married teacher, but this is played for laughs. The teacher himself is shown to be a bumbling comic character and we are invited to accept this dreadful business as being a bit of harmless fun.

The girls born between 1946 and 1964 were victims of an entrenched culture in Britain, which regarded any post-pubertal girl as being fair game for sexual fantasies or even predation. To use an exceedingly vulgar saying which was current at that time; 'Old enough to bleed, old enough to breed.' In other words, the onset of the menarche signalled a girl's availability for sexual activity. Even many grown women subscribed to this perverted view and a schoolgirl who was seduced by an adult was quite likely to find herself being blamed equally for what had happened, even by her own parents, expressions such as 'She must have led him on!' or 'It takes two to tango!' being freely tossed about in the aftermath of such situations.

The fact that they were likely to be held at least partly responsible for any abuse which they suffered acted to discourage girls from reporting anything untoward to their parents. There was another reason for this reticence. Sex was a taboo subject in many families. It was not something which most children would dream of discussing with their mother or father. If they were interfered with, then the chances were that they would not mention it to their parents; it would simply be too embarrassing for all concerned. This too goes a long way towards explaining why so much of the sexual abuse in those days remained hidden from view. Almost unbelievably, this state of affairs is also remembered with affection by those growing up in the post-war years! Here is an adult recalling the childhood days of the late 1940s, when life was so much simpler. One of the contributors to a book called *A Mobile Century*, about the changing habits of travel in Britain, was a child in the years immediately following the end of the war. She talks of how children at that time 'swam in dirty canals and played in air-raid shelters and did not tell their parents about encounters with "flashers"'. There is a lot to think about in this short statement about the way life once was for children and before we look at the idea that it might ever have been desirable for a child not to tell his or her parents about 'flashers', let us consider briefly the other two points raised.

It is certainly a debatable point as to whether swimming in dirty canals is sensible activity; we shall look in more detail at this in a later chapter. Apart from the risk of drowning, accidental deaths among the under-16s were far higher at that time: there is also the question of disease. There were no vaccinations in the late 1940s and infectious diseases such as polio were spread by contaminated water. There were definitely disadvantages too for young girls in playing in air-raid shelters. At the time of writing, Robert Black, the notorious child killer has just died in prison. Black, who was convicted of the murder of four little girls over the course of a long career of child molesting, began his offences at a very young age. In 1959, when he was just 12, he tried to rape a girl. Four years later, in 1963, he discovered a seven-year-old girl playing in a park without any adult looking after her. We have already seen that this practice of playing out alone, while beloved of many baby boomers, was sometimes fraught with hazard. So it proved in this case. The 16-year-old Black lured the child into a disused air-raid shelter, on the pretext of wishing to show her some kittens, and then attempted to strangle her. When she was unconscious, he indecently assaulted her, pushed various objects into her vagina and anus and then finished off my masturbating over his half-dead victim. By which it is seen that not all children's games in air-raid shelters ended happily.

Returning now to the question of remaining silent about abuse, we consider the final part of the statement quoted above, that children in the late 1940s 'did not tell their parents about encounters with "flashers"'. It was precisely this, that children very often did not tell their parents about sexual encounters with adults, which allowed abuse to flourish at that time. It was not only 'flashers' that children did not tell their parents about, but also overly-affectionate teachers and swimming coaches with a propensity for touching their bodies. Silence of this kind is pernicious and helps promote the sexual abuse of children. That anybody could grow misty-eyed and nostalgic about such a state of affairs is frankly incredible.

So far we have been looking at older girls, those roughly of secondary school age. Genuinely little girls, those who had not yet undergone puberty, were regarded as strictly off limits, even in the 1960s. A sharp line was generally drawn between the pursuit of the sexy little minx in a school uniform and the molestation of little girls of seven or eight. The one was a little daring; the other, utterly beyond the pale. Nevertheless, the abuse of very young children was also tolerated in the first three decades after the end of the war in a way that most of us find shocking today. Take the case of one of the commonest forms of abuse, then, as now; indecent exposure.

These days, if a man exposes his penis to a child, we take the matter pretty seriously and if it comes to light, then the police are more than likely to become involved. It was not always so. Certainly during the period we are examining, this offence and others leading on from it were often overlooked, even when children reported them. There were several reasons for this, chief of which being that 'flashing', or exposing oneself to a child, was not until 2003 classified as a sexual offence. Prosecutions were instead made under two obscure pieces of nineteenth-century legislation. One of these was the 1824 Vagrancy Act and the other the 1847 Town and Police Clauses Act.

These laws were passed not to tackle sexually-motivated exposure of a man's genitals, but rather the inadvertent sight of them consequent upon urination. Before public lavatories appeared in the middle of the nineteenth century, any convenient alley-way or secluded corner was liable to be used, principally by men, to empty their bladders. The idea that a Victorian lady might thus catch a glimpse of a man's exposed penis was felt to be very shocking and laws were needed to discourage the habit. There are still old signs fixed to the walls of London streets, bearing the legend, 'Commit No Nuisance'. This was the quaint way of warning men not to urinate in the area.

There were two consequences of this legal situation. The first was that no real statistics are available for the prevalence of this offence: they were buried among convictions for other trifling matters under the two acts, convictions relating to public health, Sunday trading and so on. There is no way of knowing which of the men who appeared in court and were subsequently convicted under the Vagrancy Act had been exposing themselves, unless a newspaper reporter happened to be present in the court. Secondly, and more seriously, the charge against those accused of indecent exposure quoted the law, which was that the man had exposed himself to 'a female', it being only women who were thought liable to be affected by such an experience. This meant that there was absolutely nothing to hinder a man showing his penis to small boys if he wished. Only girls were protected against this type of low-level abuse. Nor was this the only problem, as the law stood at that time.

Common sense tells us that the younger the victim of the 'flasher', the graver and more reprehensible the offence. What might be laughed off by a young woman of 18 could be a most distressing experience for a girl of six. In the 1950s, this was not at all how the matter was seen. Since the essence of the offence was that a 'female' might be shocked or insulted by the sight of a man's genitals, the question was seriously debated that there might be a lower age limit below which neither insult nor offence could properly be said to exist. After all, it was argued, what possible harm could be done to a girl of two if she glimpsed a man's penis? The significance of catching a fleeting glance of that part of the body would be quite lost on such a young child. What about a four- or five-year-old? The same grounds could perhaps be advanced for supposing that in such cases too, no real harm was done and the girls concerned would not be in the least shocked.

The law itself, of course, did not distinguish in this way between different ages: it was a question of the judgement made by individual magistrates when cases of this kind were brought before them. The result was that the police too used some discrimination in deciding which cases they could successfully prosecute and others which could be settled with a quiet word to the man reported for 'flashing'. This was all bound up with the perception of indecent exposure as a relatively trivial, low-level offence which was unlikely to lead to anything worse. There are to this day two schools of thought about this. Some believe that 'flashers' are essentially inadequate and harmless individuals who resort to this behaviour because they are too timid to do anything worse. Then again, there are some experts in the field who view indecent exposure as a 'trigger' offence, a warning that here is a disturbed person who might commit other and more serious sexual crimes if not deterred.

That indecent exposure *can* lead to something worse is indisputable. Such a case occurred in 1951 and the consequences were far-reaching: arrests and convictions for the indecent assault of children dropping sharply in the aftermath of what was known as the 'Clitheroe Case'. For the best part of a decade after the judgement, there was no realistic chance of gaining a conviction for the indecent assault of children, provided always that the children had been cajoled, bribed or otherwise persuaded to engage in sexual activity.

We have already looked at a number of instances of children walking to school alone or 'playing out' without the supervision of adults, noting that this often left them unprotected and at hazard from various threats, ranging from traffic accidents to homicidal maniacs. The Clitheroe Case was another of those times when the presence of a parent or other responsible adult might have averted an unpleasant situation and prevented it from developing further. In the middle of May 1951, four little girls, ranging in age from six to nine, were playing by a deserted riverbank in the Lancashire town of Clitheroe. A man appeared and began urinating into the river. This was evidently no more than a pretext for getting out his penis, because he then called over one of the girls, who was nine, and asked her to touch his penis. She did so. By good fortune, she was not afraid to tell somebody what had happened and the man was subsequently arrested and charged with indecently assaulting the child. He appeared at the local magistrates court on 24 May 1951 and the case was dismissed. The police then appealed against this decision and on 17 October 1951, the matter eventually ended up being heard before the Lord Chief Justice, Lord Goddard.

There was no doubt at all about the facts, as they had been presented. The only question to decide was whether or not what had happened to the little girl that May had been an assault. The court ruled that it had not. The three judges sitting that day were unanimous in their belief that an assault must be accompanied by hostile action of one kind or another, whether words, gestures or physical contact. In this case; nothing of the sort had happened. The man had simply asked the girl to touch him and she had done so willingly. The implications of this judgement, Fairclough v Whipp, were profound for children throughout the rest of the 1950s. In effect, the highest court in the land had ruled that molesting children was perfectly legal, as long as you could persuade them to touch you, rather than the other way round.

Modern readers might feel shocked to learn that a ruling like the one above could be made, but the law as it stood made such a decision inevitable. The Clitheroe Case was by no means the worst example of how this legal loophole left the police powerless to act against even the most disgusting offences against children. Consider a case two years later, DPP v Rogers, 1953. An 11-year-old girl was sitting in a downstairs room with her father. He came over and sat next to her, putting his arm around her shoulders. Then he led her upstairs to his bedroom; where he got her to masturbate him. Today, we find it almost inconceivable that such a course of action would turn out to be quite within the law, as it stood. Nevertheless, the father, although arrested, was acquitted when the case came to court, the precedent in the Fairclough v Whipp case being binding upon lower courts.

Anybody hoping to understand sexual abuse of children during the 1960s and 1970s, whether by famous singers and disc jockeys or merely within a normal family setting, will be quite unable to make sense of what was going on at the time, unless they are aware of the background and legal judgements such as those outlined above. Throughout most of the 1950s, adults were free to abuse children as the mood took them, always providing of course that they did so without violence or threats. The law simply could not touch such awful behaviour. It was not until the passage of the Indecency with Children Act, which came into force on 2 July 1960, that it became possible to prosecute adults for inviting children to touch them indecently. The Indecency with Children Act of 1960 was the first gender-neutral legislation in Britain designed to deal with cases of sexual abuse of children. Up until then, such offences had been strictly demarcated into those against girls and others against boys.

One factor which complicated matters relating to the sexual abuse of underage girls was that the school leaving age in Britain was, until September 1972, set at fifteen. This meant that until the 1970s, there was nothing to stop a girl who was not old enough to consent to any sort of sexual activity getting a job as a cocktail waitress, a dancer or even a striptease artiste! Those seeing what was apparently a desirable young woman in such roles might very well make an erroneous assumption about their age and maturity. A case illustrating this point with great clarity came to light at the beginning of 2016, when it was revealed that a well-known BBC disc jockey had been fired for allegedly being evasive about the circumstances of an investigation into possible sexual impropriety forty-five years earlier. In 1971, a girl whose name had been linked with that of the disc jockey was found dead of a drug overdose. She had taken her own life at the age of 15. Incredibly, this child had featured a number of times on the television programme *Top of the Pops*, where she was shown dancing on stage. The camera tended to focus upon her because she was very attractive and looked considerably older than her actual age. The line became very blurred at that time between grown women and children; a circumstance which tended to play into the hands of potential abusers. A few years earlier, another famous disc jockey, John Peel, had actually married a 15-year-old girl in the United States and then brought his bride home to Britain.

So far, we have looked only at the abuse of girls during the baby boomer years. What was the situation with boys at this time? As has been seen, one of the commonest forms of low-level abuse, the crime of indecent exposure, did not even count when carried out against male children. The difficulty about researching statistics and figures for the sexual abuse of boys is that it was enormously widespread and very little of it was recorded. It is impossible to say whether it was more common than the abuse of girls, but it was definitely regarded in a different light. In some settings, schools and scout groups spring to mind, paedophile abuse of boys was, if not accepted, then without doubt expected. The schoolmaster and scout leader with an unhealthy interest in little boys may be stereotypical figures but they are rooted firmly in historical fact. Both existed for many years and were simply a known but regrettable feature of schools and youth groups. Such men, for men they almost invariably were, were regarded as pathetic, but not particularly wicked. Often they were figures of fun, rather than objects of hatred

It seems strange to believe that the systematic abuse of young boys could ever have been thought of in this country as amusing, but it is nevertheless true. The late Arthur Marshall, broadcaster and newspaper columnist, most famous for his appearances on the television programme *Call My Bluff*, was well known as a humorous writer. In 1974 he published a book called *Girls will be Girls*, a miscellany of his writings for various magazines and newspapers. Included in the book were sketches of his childhood at a well-known boarding school. These too were written for laughs, with farcical accounts of the tribulations facing a sensitive boy at a school renowned for its sporting prowess. It is the section dealing with paedophilia which causes one to gasp with amazement today. Marshall writes that:

> Preparatory schools at that time seemed each to have its quota of unmarried masters who were still waiting for Miss Right . . . Some of them were by nature looking about for Miss Right rather less vigorously than others. Dedicated paedophiles stalked the linoleum-covered corridors and, sensing a non-frosty reception, pounced. No boy who wasn't actually repellent could consider himself safe from an amorous mauling among the rows of pendent mackintoshes.

This account relates of course to events in Arthur Marshall's own boyhood, perhaps fifty years earlier, but it is quite extraordinary that he should have been able to write in a book published in the 1970s so light-heartedly about systematic abuse of this kind. The reason was of course that paedophile teachers and scoutmasters were just as common when he was writing in 1974 as they had been during his schooldays in 1924. People knew that they existed and were abusing children on a regular basis. It was just one of those things and if a famous humourist like Arthur Marshall could see the funny side of being abused like that, well then, maybe we should too! This too is indicative of the attitudes to paedophile abuse forty or fifty years ago.

Another fascinating glimpse into the mindset of those days, indicating the widespread acceptance of the sexual abuse of children in the years at which we are looking, was provided a few years ago by the renowned and controversial biologist Richard Dawkins. He revealed that he had been abused by a teacher when he was at school in the 1950s. The language that Dawkins used to describe this awful experience is telling, indicating a similar attitude to that displayed by Arthur Marshall towards the sexual molestation to which he was routinely subjected. Richard Dawkins relates that he was pulled onto the lap of a male teacher, who then pushed his hand inside the boy's shorts and fondled his genitals. Incredibly, sixty years later, the victim of this abuse refuses to condemn the perpetrator, even now minimizing the action by describing it as 'mild touching up'.

These two accounts typify the attitude of many people until relatively recently to the abuse of schoolboys by scoutmasters, teachers, youth club leaders and others. It was felt to be, if not normal, then certainly unsurprising. Even the victims often put up with what was being done to them, viewing it perhaps as just another of those tiresome rites of passage which children and adolescents had to endure. Mercifully, this has now changed, but unless one understands the endemic sexual abuse in the decades following the end of the Second World War, then it will be altogether impossible to make sense of the attitude towards their abuse of people like Richard Dawkins. That kind of thing was the subject of jokes, rather than outrage.

To show how some sexually-motivated activity which targeted children was not taken at all seriously, even by the victims, we turn to accounts from the 1970s. Here is Arthur Marshall again, describing a visit to some public lavatories during a school trip to a cricket match:

> Our first concern, after the hour's drive, was to make for the lavatory, an open-air and rather whiffy square construction of brick, conveniently close. As we hastened in, a solitary figure drew all eyes. In a corner, and facing outwards, an aged and decrepit clergyman was standing, smiling encouragement and wildly waggling. At our fairly tender years this was a startling spectacle and one hardly knew where to look. Where not to look was plain to all. Subsequent visits found him, hope on hope ever, still there and at it.

Although this 'humorous' account was written in the 1970s about something which took place back in the 1920s, such attitudes were still very strong throughout the formative years of the baby boomers. Low-level sexual abuse of this kind was just something which happened to schoolchildren and there was no point in making a fuss about it.

As we know, exposing one's penis to little boys in this way was not even against the law when the baby boomers were growing up. Inevitably, this immunity from the law led inexorably to some men going even further, confident in the knowledge that their actions would probably not even be regarded as a criminal offence. From showing their penis to a boy, it was only a short step to masturbating in his presence. A boy sitting alone in a cinema might find a man coming and sitting next to him, who, as soon as the lights went down, would take out his penis and begin playing with himself. Very few boys would have even thought of telling their parents about such a thing in those days.

The 1950s and 1960s were certainly a golden age for those who wished to indulge in the sexual abuse of children. Some of this abuse, exposing oneself to a boy for instance, was not even illegal and for the whole of 1950s it was not even against the law to persuade a little girl to masturbate you. Combined with the legal situation was the fact that most children would not have told any adult about abuse, even when it was of the grossest and most unpleasant kind. Sex was something which was off-limits as a topic of conversation in the average family. After encountering the man who was, we are given to understand from Arthur Marshall's account, masturbating in front of schoolboys, not one of them reported the matter to a member of staff. As the author went on to say, 'Instinct told us not to discuss the matter with Matron . . .' During the first two or three decades following the end of the Second World War, it was quite common for all the pupils in a school to know which of the teachers was a pervert, but for parents and staff to be completely in the dark. Both girls and boys would warn each other of the perils of being alone with this or that PE or music teacher, and yet the information never reached an adult.

When it did became apparent, as happened from time to time, to a school, scout group, church or other organization that one of the adults working for them had an unhealthy interest in children, the chief emotion felt by all parties was embarrassment. Nobody wished to make a distasteful fuss and the commonest mechanism for handling the problem was that of a discrete word being spoken to the person concerned, who then went off quietly, often to join another youth club, athletics association or whatever, where he could then continue his predations against little boys or girls. Until very recently, this was almost invariably regarded as the most satisfactory means of tackling a very unfortunate and awkward situation. It was felt to be in nobody's interest, least of all the children concerned, to see the matter dragged through the courts. All of which made it very easy and satisfying to pursue a career of child molesting during the years at which we are looking.

Even if a report *was* made to the police and resulted in a court case, as did happen from time to time, the chances were that any conviction would only be registered at the local magistrates' court, rather than finding its way to the Criminal Records Department of Scotland Yard. Providing that the case was not reported in the local newspaper, there was every possibility that the offender would be able to move from the scout group where he had carried out the abuse and simply begin running the local church youth club or helping out at the air cadets or some other location which would give him access to children. In this way, men at that time were able to abuse children for many years with complete impunity. Sometimes, a case *would* reach the papers, necessitating a move to another town which gave a fresh start and the continuation of sexual abuse, perhaps under a different name.

Following a number of well-publicised murders, including that of two little girls at Soham in 2002 by a school caretaker about whom insufficient enquiries had been made before allowing him unlimited access to children, matters changed dramatically and anybody working with or having regular access to children was required to undergo background checks, including a search for convictions at the Criminal Records Bureau (CRB). This made it very difficult, indeed next to impossible, to conceal a murky past which included convictions for, or even suspicions of, sexual activity with a child. One might think that nobody in his or her senses could possibly object to moves designed to prevent predatory paedophiles from gaining access to new victims, but one would be quite wrong. There was enormous opposition to the new system when it was first introduced. Baby boomers who had grown up at a time when the sexual abuse of children was a constant background in their lives were, surprisingly, in the vanguard of the struggle to ensure that child molesters continued to enjoy easy and unrestricted access to their prey. Admitting that abuse was distressingly common when they were children would have run the risk of tainting the fantasy world which many of them had constructed and it was easier to object to the process of CRB checks as just one more aspect of the 'Nanny State'. Rules and regulations dealing with adults working with or coming into regular contact with children are often dismissed as unnecessary red tape by older people who should know better. To understand the point, it will be necessary to look in some detail at an unappetising topic, that of what child molesters actually *did* to their young victims in the 1950s and 1960s.

With modern, twenty-first century attitudes to sex, there is a tendency to assume that sexual activity almost invariably entails genital contact. This was not at all the case sixty years ago, especially where child molesting was concerned. Often, the activity took place while the adult participant at least was fully clothed. What Arthur Marshall described as 'amorous mauling among the rows of pendent mackintoshes' provides us with a good example of this type of thing, the technical name of which is frottage. Even in the old days at which we are looking, the sight of a naked teacher or scout leader fooling around with a child might have been expected to raise eyebrows a little, and so much of the abuse was conducted by means of men rubbing themselves, fully clothed, against the children in whom they had a sexual interest. This could be done in the course of play-fighting, tickling, sport, seemingly innocuous cuddles or while a child was seated on the man's lap. This activity gave the adult perverts a pleasurable thrill and could even result in orgasm, given the right circumstances. There is a very detailed and appallingly accurate passage in Vladimir Nabokov's novel *Lolita* which describes precisely how this process takes place. Humbert Humbert, the protagonist, has manipulated a 12-year-old girl into laying across his lap. This gives him an opportunity to rub his clothed genitals against her body for some time, until he 'crushed out against her left buttock the longest ecstasy man or monster had ever known'.

The practice of frottage, sometimes known as 'dry humping', was one of the commonest types of sexual abuse carried out against children. There were a number of advantages from the point of view of the abuser, chief of which was that there was always an element of what might not inaptly be termed 'plausible deniability'. In cadet units and scouts troops, there was often play-fighting and rough games in which an adult might join in without anybody remarking on it as being peculiar. This gave some men the chance to rub their groins against young boys, thus gaining sexual satisfaction. The same end might be achieved with young children by hugging them, teaching them sports, showing how to hold a musical instrument or sitting them on one's lap. At the end of such an episode, even the child might not be sure just what had been going on and to spectators, the whole thing might look like a bit of harmless rough and tumble, with a grown man entering into the spirit of children's play with a refreshing and charming lack of self-consciousness. This is another way in which the abuse of children could take place, quite literally 'in plain sight'.

Most British baby boomers will know about the practices outlined above, which makes it all the more mysterious that some of them are still seemingly opposed to putting an end to the conditions which allowed child abuse like this to flourish for so many years. Whenever any change relating to people's safety is proposed, a new regulation or law which prohibits or restricts some supposed liberty which was previously enjoyed, some baby boomer may always be relied upon to raise the cry of 'Health and Safety gone mad!' or 'The Nanny State!' Sure enough, when attempts began to be made to limit physical activity between adults and children, by suggesting that the less grown-ups rubbed their bodies against those of little boys and girls the better it would be, this too was denounced as a pernicious interference in the natural relations which should exist between the generations. Frank Furedi, the well-known professor of sociology, even wrote a book on the subject. The subtitle of this book, *Licensed to Hug*, was *How child protection policies are poisoning the relationship between the generations and damaging the voluntary sector.*

The psychology of the baby boomers which leads them to adopt such a strange attitude towards the protection of children from sexual predators is curious and we shall be seeing other examples later on in this book. Essentially, the position held by many older people in Britain is that their own childhoods were pretty well perfect and should be held up as the model for modern childhood. If children today are not getting as much exercise as they did themselves or are eating more than children did at a similar age in 1955, then there is something wrong. In the same way, if children today are slumped in their bedrooms chatting on the Internet for hours, instead of queuing up outside a red telephone box, then this must mean that childhood today is somehow disordered and in need of repair. Any deviation from the childhood pattern of the 1950s and 1960s is automatically seen as a change for the worse.

This peculiar frame of mind leads to government initiatives intended to encourage children to walk to school, as they did sixty years ago, and eat a healthier diet, as was allegedly once the case. Childhood in the days when the baby boomers were growing up is the ideal to aim at. Unfortunately, as we saw in the last chapter, the memory of our own childhood is not an infallible guide to how things really were when we were little. The idea that an awful lot of children were being sexually abused or even murdered by lust-driven paedophiles does not accord with the image of a supposedly gentler, safer and more civilized era and so is subconsciously rejected by many older people. This in turn means that all these CRB checks and vetting is viewed as a lot of expensive and time wasting nonsense; the only practical effect of which is stopping adults from cuddling a distressed child.

Furedi's book *Licensed to Hug* promotes the notion, popular among baby boomers, that safeguarding is pretty pointless. In a chapter entitled 'Child Protection and "No Touch" Policies', Furedi, himself of course a baby boomer, suggests that policies formulated by official bodies or voluntary organizations to discourage adults from pressing their bodies against children are unnecessary and in fact harmful to children. He quotes research by academics at Manchester Metropolitan University into 'the problematic of touching between children and professionals'. This was said to explore 'the tension between children's need for nurturing contact and the fear that such contact may be interpreted as abuse'. Among the ideas at which this study looked were, 'minimizing cuddling young children, even requiring particular ways of doing this, such as the sideways cuddle (to avoid any full-frontal contact)'. The thrust of *Licensed to Hug*, which many older professionals working with children thought to be a long-overdue exposé of Health and Safety madness, is that worrying about physical contact with small children is largely a lot of fuss about nothing. Ideas such as the 'sideways cuddle' are mentioned in such a way as to suggest that only somebody looking for risks where there were none to be found would even consider something so bizarre. In fact of course, the whole aim of the sideways cuddle is to minimize opportunities for what Arthur Marshall called 'amorous mauling'. Pressing their bodies, especially for obvious reasons the groin area, against children's bodies has always been a mainstay of paedophiles who are unable to get a child alone, this manoeuvre being quite possible to undertake in public in the context of a music or sports lesson. Anything which discourages adults working with children from rubbing their groins against children in this way is surely to be welcomed, rather than ridiculed.

What is interesting and perhaps significant is that children and young people themselves see very well why such rules are in place. The younger a person, the less likely they are to object to policies of this sort which are designed to protect children from covert abuse. By and large, the only people who grow impatient about or mock such initiatives are baby boomers, many of whom have in the years since their childhood managed to forget how common sexual abuse of this kind once was.

We have looked in detail at one of the less appetising aspects of childhood during the baby boomer years. In the next chapter, the idea will be examined that crime, including murder, and anti-social behaviour, by children is a relatively new phenomenon and one which indicates that something is wrong with modern society.

Chapter 3

Of Moral Panics and ASBOs:
Juvenile Crime and Disorder in the 1950s and 1960s

It is one thing to listen tolerantly to the reminiscences of older people, while treating their anecdotes with a certain amount of reserve; it is quite another when those same flawed memories are used as the basis for legislation which will affect every one of us! This, unfortunately, is what has been happening in Britain in recent years. Baby boomers and their admirers in the government and legislature are looking with jaundiced eyes upon the modern world and when they find that it seems to differ too radically from the past, as they believe it to have been, they put together guidance or try and pass laws which will, they hope, rectify the situation; in other words, to turn back the clock. In case anybody should think this a fanciful assertion, it might be pointed out that Anti-Social Behaviour Orders, more commonly known as ASBOs, are a direct consequence of this bizarre process.

There is in this country a widespread view that children and young people are less respectful of authority, more badly behaved, wilder and more prone to disorderly and anti-social conduct than was once the case. Instead of playing Cowboys and Indians in the park, they now spend their days hanging round shopping centres, wearing hoodies and menacing respectable citizens. Some of them are even being arrested for firearms-related offences, something which would have been unheard of a few years ago. This at least is the perception of many middle-aged and elderly people. From time to time, acts of savagery are committed by these modern children which appear, on the face of it, to be quite unprecedented. This has resulted in the expression 'feral youths' being coined, to describe children and teenagers who apparently behave more like wild animals than young human beings. All of which leads a lot of people to conclude that there has for years been something disordered and injurious about British society; that it in some way causes children to go wrong and carry on like savage beasts. Take, for example, the murder of toddler James Bulger.

In 1993, two 10-year-old boys abducted little James Bulger from a

Liverpool shopping centre. Once they were alone with him, the youngsters killed the child by inflicting forty-two wounds on him and leaving his body on a railway line. So shocking was the murder of this defenceless child that a number of politicians used the case to draw conclusions about the state of a society which could produce such dysfunctional children. The then Shadow Home Secretary, Tony Blair, referred to this crime by talking of, 'the ugly manifestations of a society that is becoming unworthy of that name'. The overall impression was that here was a uniquely awful incident which told us something about the shortcomings of modern Britain; at least as far as the way children were growing up was concerned.

More recently, a 10-year-old boy called Damilola Taylor died in London after being assaulted by two brothers, one 12 and the other 13 years of age. Damilola bled to death after an artery was severed. This too was treated as a dreadful example of how vicious and depraved some children have become in recent years. How very different from the way things used to be in the 1950s, when the worst crimes that a child might be accused of were likely to be trespassing or perhaps setting off a firework in the street. This at least was the popular view of such crimes. The idea of a 10- or 12-year-old boy killing another child in those days was beyond all belief! The reality, as experienced by the baby boomers themselves, was somewhat different.

The notion of 'Broken Britain' or our 'broken society' has become a popular one since David Cameron became Prime Minister in 2010 and the *Sun*, which backed his premiership, has used these expressions repeatedly. Following the 2011 riots in English cities, Cameron talked of the 'moral collapse' of British society, singling out such causes as children without fathers and schools without discipline. It was plain that he was contrasting modern society with that of his youth, where children *did* have fathers and there was discipline in the schools.

This whole idea, that youngsters today are out of control and in danger of becoming 'feral', is a classic example of a moral panic and the creation of a folk devil. Both expressions might need a little explanation. Moral panics occur when a large number of people start to believe that there is some threat to the stability or well-being of the society in which they live. Sometimes the anxiety is about muggers or paedophiles; at others it centres around violent computer games or the use of drugs. Such panics are whipped up by the mass media and frequently exploited by politicians. This is why both the *Sun* and successive Prime Ministers have been keen on promoting the idea of Britain's 'broken society'. An integral part of most moral panics is the creation of folk devils, people who can be identified as posing a danger to ordinary citizens. These can be drug pushers', satanic abusers, illegal immigrants, human traffickers or a variety of other bogeymen. For some while, the most popular folk devil has been the feral youths or hoodies who frequent our streets with a view to stealing, taking drugs, fighting or even committing murder. The moral panic which centres around wild and undisciplined children and youths was created by explicitly comparing the supposed behaviour of many children today with how, it was claimed, things used to be when the baby boomers were young and there were no feral youths around.

As a matter of fact, ghastly murders of children, by other children, were just as much a feature of life during the formative years of the baby boomers as they are now. It is just that such horrors have been conveniently forgotten, airbrushed from history if you like, to avoid spoiling the attractive, *Swallows and Amazons*-style world that many older people claim to have inhabited as children. Let us look now at a concrete example, one which also shows the folly of letting young children play outdoors without adult supervision, something which we are assured by some baby boomers is a wise and good thing to allow children to engage in. We shall see how games of Cowboys and Indians in a park sometimes ended in the period at which we are looking, by examining a real incident, which began with a bunch of nine- and ten-year-olds going to their local park to play.

In 1960 it was, as we are frequently reminded, very common for children to be sent out to play by themselves, with no adult accompanying them. This helped them to develop independence and also ensured that they got plenty of fresh air and exercise and did not become overweight. What could possibly be bad about that? On the afternoon of Saturday, 20 February 1960, a number of children were playing Cowboys and Indians in Mayfield Park in the southern English city of Southampton. One of them was nine-year-old Iris Dawkins. There were no adults with them. At about three that afternoon, Iris fell off a plank bridge and became covered in mud. She decided to go home and change her soaked clothes. A woman

living in a house next to the park saw a child whom she believed to be
Iris, walking away from the stream, accompanied by a boy of about the
same age. This was the last time that she was seen alive.

When Iris Dawkins was found dead, later that day, it was at once seen
that she had been the victim of a frenzied attack by somebody armed with
a knife; the little girl had been stabbed no fewer than thirty-eight times.
Although about 150 people were watching a game of football in one part
of Mayfield Park that afternoon, no adults had been seen in the area where
the children had been playing and the child had last been seen in the
company of a boy of 9 or 10. The police therefore focused their attentions
on other children who had been in the park that afternoon. They found a
10-year-old boy who not only admitted having been with Iris on the
afternoon that she died, but also made a statement in which he said that:

> I think Iris fell over . . . I might have been playing with a knife at the
> time. I fell on top of her. I think the knife went into her shoulder. I
> had a knife in my hand. The blade was open a little way. I may have
> stuck it in her more than once. I cannot remember now. She was lying
> down, her eyes were open and she was breathing normally. I thought
> she was playing. I said 'Cheerio' and went away.

It will perhaps come as no surprise that after making this statement, the
boy was charged with murder. The headline from the report on this case
may be seen in Illustration 10.

This then was a case very like that of James Bulger and yet it has
become lost to memory. The similarities are really quite eerie, even down
to the way that the newspapers tried to lay the blame for the murder on
the supposedly baleful influence of new forms of entertainment. It will be
recalled that during the trial of the boys accused of killing James Bulger
reference was made to a videotape of the film *Child's Play 3; Chucky's
Revenge*. It was suggested that watching this film might have inspired
some of the acts of brutality inflicted on the helpless child. There were
even calls to ban the film. Back in 1960, newspapers made much of the
fact that the boy who was tried for Iris Dawkins' murder watched people
being stabbed on television thrillers. In one of his statements, he said that
'I got excited and stuck it in her. Then I got frightened. I have seen
stabbing on television and next week you see them in another part. I watch

all the murders. I like the way they track them down and question them.' The fact that a 10-year-old boy talked of watching 'all the murders' on television and of seeing stabbing, led some people to blame television for the murder, just as there are those today who blame violent computer games or the Internet for juvenile crimes of violence. Although the judge at his trial ruled that there was no case to answer, due to procedural irregularities during the police investigation, the boy was eventually convicted of the murder nine years later after making a confession.

Here then is a concrete instance of what the unsupervised playing of Cowboys and Indians could lead to a little over half a century ago. From an activity such as one might find in the pages of *Just William*, the scene descends swiftly into something out of *Lord of the Flies*! It is not of course being suggested that murders of this sort were a common occurrence during the 1950s and 1960s, any more than they are now. What is definitely true though is that such cases were no less frequent than they are today. As far back as one cares to look in British history, there have been children who commit murder. In the early fifteenth century, the death in England was recorded of a five-year-old girl. She had been shot dead by a 10-year-old boy armed with a bow and arrow. Or take William Allnutt from the London district of Hackney, who in 1847, at the age of 12, poisoned his grandfather by sprinkling arsenic on his food. He was sentenced to death, although later reprieved. His case resonates with the trial of another baby boomer at the Old Bailey in 1962. In 1961 and 1962, 14-year-old Graham Young poisoned his father, sister, stepmother and one of his school friends. His stepmother died and when he appeared at the Old Bailey, the diminutive schoolboy was sent to Broadmoor. There were other schoolboys in those early years of the 1960s who tried to kill people. In the same month that Iris Dawkins was murdered, a 15-year-old boy in Leeds was charged with the attempted murder of a little boy of five. He admitted having tied the child up, gagged him and then trying to strangle him. He had done the same thing to an eight-year-old. Again, it is not to be supposed that the 1960s were one long succession of murders and attempted murders by children and teenagers, merely that such things happened in those days just as much as they do today.

By editing out the gory and distressing parts of the post-war years, the baby boomers have more or less succeeded in creating a wholly fictitious world where children could play safely and with their innocence preserved. Such a time existed in the 1960s no more than in the 1860s or 1760s. There have always been vicious and depraved children and as they grow older, these children sometimes turn to murder. Where the 1950s and 1960s differ from other periods is that many of the ugly and distressing things concerning children which took place at that time have been forgotten, almost as though they have been deliberately and carefully erased from history. This meant that when an event such as the murder of James Bulger took place thirty years later, it was regarded as a manifestation of what some called the 'moral vacuum' at the heart of modern, British society.

Viewing the murder committed by two 10-year-old boys as being something unheard of and a product of a 'broken' society had far-reaching effects. The generation of politicians who came to power with Tony Blair in 1997 had been working on the assumption that something would have to be done to roll back what they saw as the tide of anti-social behaviour by children which led, in extreme cases, to the sort of thing which had happened to James Bulger. Here had been truanting children, hanging round a shopping centre with nothing to do but get into trouble. Surely, a new law would be able to put a stop to that sort of thing?

This whole idea, of a law to control wayward children and ultimately prevent tragedies such as that which had befallen the two-year-old boy in Liverpool, was predicated on the notion that the murder of one child by another was an unheard-of aberration; something which could not have happened when Tony Blair, himself of course a baby boomer, was a child. The result was the 1998 Crime and Disorder Act, which introduced the new mechanism of ASBOs to prevent young tearaways from making a nuisance of themselves, and even committing murder, in the future. The distorted perception of the post-war years had far-reaching consequences with which we still live: although ASBOs were abolished in 2015, a similar mechanism still exists.

One more instance of child-murder by other children should be enough to make the point. We have seen a number of reasons why children being out and about on the streets without an adult to look after them are at increased hazard, despite the supposedly beneficial long-term effects of such freedom. Had Iris Dawkins been with her mother or father, it is exceedingly unlikely that she would have been murdered on that fateful Saturday afternoon in 1960. Some of the children we have seen come to harm through being out and about by themselves have really been very young indeed. In Chapter 1, for instance, we looked at five-year-old Diana Tift who was snatched from the street while walking alone to her grandmother's house in December 1965. Children younger than that were allowed out alone though. So it was that when, on the afternoon of 25 May 1968, four-year-old Martin Brown went alone into a sweetshop in the Scotswood district of Newcastle-upon-Tyne; Wilson Dixon, who served him, thought nothing more about it once the little boy had left the shop. A four-year-old visiting the shops by himself simply wasn't a remarkable or noteworthy occurrence in those days. The brief sighting by a shop assistant on that Saturday afternoon, almost fifty years ago, was the last time that anybody other than his killer saw Martin Brown alive. Later that day, the little boy's body was found in a derelict house near the sweetshop. There were no marks on the dead child and no reason to suspect foul play. An open verdict was returned at the subsequent inquest.

Two months later an even younger child was out without an adult. Brian Howe was just three years old. He was lured to a piece of waste ground by two girls, one of whom was 11 and the other 13. There, the child was strangled and his corpse mutilated. An attempt was made to skin his penis with a razor blade. Eventually the girls were arrested for Brian Howe's murder and it then became clear that Martin Brown had also died after being abducted and attacked by one or both of the two children implicated in the killing and mutilation of Brian Howe. The younger of the two children had been 10 when Martin Brown died.

At the subsequent trial, the older of the children was acquitted, but 11-year-old Mary Bell was convicted of the manslaughter of both of the little boys. The first killing had taken place the day before her 11th birthday. Crimes of this sort by children are as uncommon today as they were in the 1960s, but to suggest that they are *more* common, or that the murder of a little boy by 10-year-olds tells us anything useful about the state of our society, are both untrue. At all times in British history, there have been children who feel the need or desire to kill other children. This was the case during the 1950s and 1960s, just as much as it is in today's 'Broken Britain'. Four-year-old Martin Brown was of course one of the last of the baby boomers to be born and one of those whose memories of playing out until teatime we will not be reading about.

It has been claimed that one of the most frightening aspects of modern youth culture in Britain is the supposed propensity for boys and youths to carry, and even on occasion use, knives. The suggestion is made that this problem is now endemic in certain parts of the country, especially the big cities. In 2015, the law was changed, so that anybody found carrying a knife in a public place would, after a second conviction, face a mandatory prison sentence. This became known as the 'Second strike and you're out' policy. Just as with the creation of the mechanism for dishing out ASBOs, this law was in response to a perceived problem which our legislators saw as being new and alarming. It is not necessary for anything to be done with the knife; it is enough that it is being carried around in somebody's pocket. Draconian measures of this sort are felt necessary to tackle what is sometimes known as the 'knife culture'. The carrying of a knife is one of the commonest reasons for exclusion from school and even primary schools are now having to take steps actively to detect and deter pupils from carrying knives.

All of which sounds most worrying and you would be hard-pressed to find any responsible adult who is not in favour of strong measures being taken to tackle this apparent scourge. Knives in primary schools, indeed! What is the world coming to? Once again, we see laws being drawn up which are predicated on the faulty memories of older people and those who listen to them, who wish to restore the world to the prelapsarian state of innocence which supposedly existed during the youth of the baby boomers. Perhaps it would help if we examined a country in the grip of a genuine knife culture and see what lessons might be drawn from it.

Imagine, if you will, a time when practically every schoolboy in the land owns or carries a knife. The possession of edged weapons is an accepted fact of life and parents even encourage this unhealthy state of affairs by buying knives and giving them to their sons for birthday and Christmas presents. This knife culture is even reinforced by the Church. Cathedrals across the country sell knives for children in their souvenir shops, with pictorial representations of the cathedral on their hilts. Knives are one of the most popular items for children to bring back from holidays at the seaside. The largest youth organization in the country encourages members openly to wear sheath knives on their belts. In schools, games involving the throwing and brandishing of knives are enormously popular among pupils, even for those below the age of 11. Incredibly, teachers smile indulgently at all this, tolerating the display of weapons. The police make no attempt to discourage the carrying of knives, taking it for granted that most boys will have one in their possession, either at school or in the street.

This imaginary excursion has taken us not to some remote and dysfunctional foreign country nor to a strange and dystopian future, but rather back to the cosy, childhood world of the British baby boomers. In those days, one would have been hard-pressed to find a boy who did not own several penknives, some with razor-sharp blades four or five inches long. Many of these were souvenirs from the seaside or school trips, with gaily-coloured coats of arms or depictions of townscapes, castles or cathedrals and so on covering the handles. In Illustration 7 we see such a knife, a souvenir from the seaside.

The penknife was for many years an integral feature of British boyhood. These knives, which are known sometimes as pocket knives, were originally devised, as the name suggests, to be carried on the person and used for sharpening quills into serviceable pens. Even when the nib had been carved, it was still prone to getting twisted or mangled during writing and so it was necessary to mend it from time to time. A folding knife which could be safely carried in the pocket was the very thing for this.

Because it had such innocuous origins, associated with learning and literacy, the penknife was not viewed in the same way as other knives. A youth armed with a Bowie knife might be up to no good, but having a penknife in one's pocket was viewed in quite a different light. Due to the various attachments with which penknives typically came, they were often seen as useful tools, rather than knives *per se*. Bottle and can openers, little saws, screwdrivers, the thing for getting stones out of horses' hoofs; the list of supplementary gadgets on a good penknife was endless. At the heart of the thing though, its very *raison d'être* one might say, was a sharp blade.

When debate in the press turns to the subject of knife crime, it is as well to recall the state of affairs which once existed in this country regarding the carrying of knives by children and young people, for it helps to put modern views in context. Worries about the carrying of blades and the legislation which has imposed such savage penalties on the practice of boys having knives in their pockets are all based on the assumption that children today are somehow different and far more ungovernable and wild than those of sixty years ago. It might have been safe for those who are now members of the judiciary or who sit in the legislature to carry knives around all the time when they were youngsters, but such a state of affairs can certainly not be tolerated with today's youth! Why, there's no telling what they'll get up to with the things; they'll be stabbing each other to death all over the place. Once again, we see the myth clearly set out that children today are different from those of their parents and grandparents generation. Children in the 1950s could be trusted with edged weapons, but that was because they were a different breed. These days, young people are not to be relied upon to act sensibly and laws have to be passed to ensure that they cannot even buy so much as a butter knife until they are able to prove with photographic evidence that they are at least 21 years of age. Times have changed and nobody wishes to see schoolboys with knives in their pockets, which because the inferior and degraded sate of modern youth now represents a clear and present danger to others.

Of course, it was not only penknives which were carried by children in the past. Boy Scouts often carried larger sheath knives, which they wore at their hips. When attending camp or sometimes out and about on other events, it was quite the thing for scouts to have fearsome-looking knives dangling from their belts. These sometimes had ornamental handles and were definite status symbols, the boys boasting of who had the largest or sharpest knife.

Larger knives were expensive and were often given by parents or uncles as Christmas or birthday presents. These knives, and others of various kinds, were played with, used to sharpen pencils, brandished, displayed and sometimes used to inflict injuries or even mortal wounds on other children. It was common for boys to have a whole collection of knives knocking about in their rooms; souvenirs from school trips, sheath knives from when they were in the Scouts, large penknives with a dozen blades, old army clasp knives that some relative who had been in the forces had passed on to them and half a dozen other types. Knives were a background to baby boomer boyhood.

Knives had many purposes, other than just being used for whittling sticks. They were often used in games in the school playground or park. Here is an example of the sort of game commonly played by schoolboys, and sometimes girls, in the 1950s and 1960s. The object of Splits, as the name suggests, was to cause your opponent actually to perform the splits and then try to stretch his legs even further. Two people stood facing each other, one of them holding a knife. A penknife could be used for this; but sheath knives or even a kitchen knives were not unknown. In short, children at primary school would sometimes smuggle their mother's bread knife into a primary school.

The first person would throw the knife, so that it stuck into the ground near their opponent's feet. If it did not stick in by the blade, then this go did not count; the knife had therefore to be hurled down with great force. If it did stick in, then the other person would need to place his foot where the knife was and it was then his turn. Accidents were inevitable and it was not altogether unknown for children to end up with knife wounds to their feet or shins! In essence, the game was a little like twister and the wonder of it is that not one adult ever seemed to find anything disturbing or even unusual about seeing children playing with blades in this way.

Here is another popular game involving knives, one which resulted in many minor injuries and not a few visits to the casualty department of the local hospital. Girls had clapping and skipping games, which involved clapping or jumping over a skipping rope to a rhythm, usually accompanied by some chanted rhyme. No boy would have been seen dead playing such games, but they had their own version of games involving rhythmic movements, which used knives or other sharp implements such as dividers or compasses. In its simplest form, this game consisted of spreading one's left hand on a desk or, if outdoors, on the grass and then stabbing round the outstretched fingers as fast as one dared; the object being or course to avoid chopping off a finger in the process. Sometimes, more complex patterns would be attempted. The boy might stab first between the first two fingers, then the next two and then back to the first pair and so on. This required great dexterity and cool nerves. Of course, all the boys wished to show that they were quicker and more adept at their use of the knife than any of the others present, and so there was always the need to go faster and engage in more complicated patterns than anybody else in the group. It was very rare for a game of this sort not to end ultimately in bloodshed!

These days, stabbing games such as the one above are more likely to be carried out with felt-tip pens, rather than knives or dividers, which may not be a bad a thing at all. The reason for going into a little detail about knives and the part they played in the average baby boomer boy's life has been to demonstrate that there was a genuine and pervasive knife culture at that time, which appears to have vanished from their collective memory. This interest in knives extended into children's fiction. William Brown and his friends, from Richmal Crompton's *Just William* stories, were enthusiastic carriers of knives. William's parents gave him a knife for a Christmas present and when he went to stay with a relative, he was presented with a Burmese sheath knife by a retired army officer. Knives feature in quite a few of the William stories.

Even in girls' school fiction, knives make an appearance as quite an unremarkable part of everyday life among children. *Autumn Term*, a school story by Antonia Forest published in 1948, has as its protagonist 12-year-old Nicola Marlow. She goes off to boarding school, taking with a her a knife with no fewer than sixteen blades. This is openly displayed and none of the pupils nor staff bat an eyelid at the thought of such a young child waving the thing about! Fictional it may have been, but in real life too, there was a general assumption by teachers that boys, and sometimes girls, would be carrying knives. If some minor job in the classroom required a screwdriver, for instance, the teacher might well ask if anybody had a penknife handy, whereupon a dozen boys would volunteer theirs. A boy who never carried a knife during the baby boomer era would have been regarded as something of an oddity.

The inevitable riposte from baby boomers at this point will be that although penknives and other weapons might have been used for such harmless pursuits as whittling sticks and sharpening pencils, children in those days certainly would never have dreamed of sticking the things in each other with deadly intent, the way that they do these days. Again, we encounter a peculiar type of false memory syndrome. Stabbings by and against children and young people *did* occur regularly in the 1950s, 1960s and 1970s, just as they do today. Knives taken to school were used as weapons, sometimes to deadly effect. This point will perhaps be illuminated if we examine some specific cases of this sort of thing from that time.

We have already seen how Iris Dawkins was hacked to death during a game of Cowboys and Indians. This murder was carried out by a schoolboy wielding an ordinary penknife. In December of that same year, 1960, 13-year-old John Day was taken to hospital in Tilbury after being stabbed in the course of a fight in a school playground. Knives were being used by youths on the streets that month, as well as in school playgrounds. Two weeks after John Day was stabbed at school, 17-year-old Keith Muncy was stabbed to death in a street fight. The 16-year-old boy who was charged with his murder apparently accused the dead boy of staring at him.

The remarkable thing about knife crime among young people during the 1960s is that it did not make the headlines, being viewed as not especially newsworthy. The stabbing of 13-year-old John Day rated only four lines in the *Times*, appearing in the 'other news' section. An increase of a halfpenny in the price of a loaf of bread was evidently seen as more important, this item appearing before news of the school stabbing. Here is another school stabbing, this time from 1963. A 13-year-old boy at a school in Old Trafford stabbed a fellow pupil during a lesson, 'to make him jump'. At Manchester County Juvenile Court, he was put on probation for two years.

Some of this schoolboy knife crime was more serious than simply jabbing a fellow pupil and leaving a superficial wound. In 1966, PC Brian Armstrong was stabbed to death in Gateshead while questioning a 14-year-old schoolboy. The child was later charged with the police officer's murder. The weapon used was the traditional schoolboy's penknife. Just imagine the conclusions which would be drawn about the terrible state of childhood in the modern world if we read in tomorrow's newspaper about a policeman being stabbed to death by a schoolboy! Throughout the 1960s, knife crime among children and young people came in waves. In May 1968, 15-year-old Clive Chambers was stabbed during a playground fight at Holloway Boys' School in North London. A boy of the same age was arrested after the incident. The following month, 13-year-old Joseph Gil was stabbed in the playground of St Bonaventure's School. Another pupil at the school appeared in court, charged with wounding. There is not enough space to list every such case from the period at which we are looking, but it is perhaps enough to note that knives were being carried and used as weapons by children and young people, both at school and in the streets. One final example will show how serious were some of these incidents of knife crime, which took place against the background of what can only be described as a 'knife culture'. At Wandsworth Comprehensive School in South London in 1971, 14-year-old Lee Selmes was stabbed to death in a fight. Another 14-year-old pupil was charged with his murder.

It may be objected that offences such as those above were rarities during the 1960s, whereas today they are commonplace. This is a fair point and leads us neatly to a point made earlier in this book; the difficulties encountered when trying to prove that this or that phenomenon is increasing, decreasing or, as is often suggested of knife crime, reaching epidemic proportions. Obviously, newspapers do not report every incident of the use of knives at school and so we must look elsewhere if we wish to discover an objective estimate of the rate of such crimes. We can hardly rely upon the memories of those who were themselves children at the time, because as we have seen, there is a distinct tendency to play down any unfavourable aspect of childhood in the distant past. Perhaps we can turn to the records from the courts or the Home Office? Here we come to the problem of analysing and examining statistics from the past which might have been gathered or recorded in different ways than they are now. In this instance, the possibility of establishing how many children were being stabbed or convicted of wounding or killing others with knives in the 1960s and then comparing these data with those being collected today, is remote in the extreme.

For one thing, only in the last few years has the Home Office begun to collect the figures for how many people are stabbed each year in Britain. This is of course because 'stabbing' is no more a specific criminal offence than is 'mugging', another offence whose incidence is hard to determine. Statistics often relate to what the police call 'knife-enabled crime', which covers domestic murders, robberies and a host of other things. Not all the crimes in this catch-all category actually involve people being injured by knives. If a boy robs somebody by threatening him with a knife, that too is listed as a 'knife-enabled crime'. During the 1950s and 1960s, the use of a knife might be mentioned in the original charge, but actual convictions were listed as offences such as causing Grievous Bodily Harm and so on. Without trawling through the records of every court in the country, it is therefore impossible even to hazard a guess as to how many stabbings were being carried out by or against children. All that we can state with certainty is that such things were taking place during the 1960s, just as they are today. There are also indications, from the amount of news coverage given to these cases, that they were not regarded as being as serious fifty years ago as they are now.

The above crimes involving the use of knives by schoolboys are mainly from the 1960s, but as far back as one cares to look, the same kind of thing may be found. On 24 June 1954, for instance, a Shepherds Bush schoolboy was sent to an approved school when he appeared at the West London Juvenile Court. It was stated that he had been running what the prosecution described as a 'protection racket' at the school he attended. When four boys refused to pay up, he carved his initials onto their arms with a penknife. It is the same however far back we look in our quest for the mythical world of wholesome, happy and uncomplicated childhood. In every age, there are schoolboys and schoolgirls who behave in savage and violent ways. Whenever we see such things, for example in the murder of James Bulger or Damilola Taylor, we are shocked and try to persuade ourselves that this never used to happen in the old days and that something must in recent years have gone wrong with society to breed such monsters. Just to underline the point, let us look back to the halcyon era of the years 'before the war'. Let's take a random twelve-month period and see what turns up.

In the quiet Cheshire town of Nantwich in February 1926, a schoolboy was stabbed in the back by another pupil. The wounding apparently resulted from two other boys pretending to fight each other with penknives and the injured schoolboy simply got in the way. Less than a year later, in Castleford, a town in the north of England, two schoolboys stole a couple of penknives from a shop. They then walked down the street, stabbing girls in the legs as they went. The boys were later charged with unlawful wounding. In that same month, January 1927, a 14-year-old schoolboy called Arthur Edward Shillibeer appeared at the Old Bailey in London, charged with murdering a 13-year-old boy by stabbing him. This was a gang-related killing. A group of boys in the south London district of

Bermondsey, all aged between 12 and 15, were terrorising the neighbourhood by their violent activities. Eleven of the gang cornered Arthur Shillibeer and in defence he took out his penknife and used it to kill the leader of the gang. Because of the nature of the crime, the charge of murder was dropped and a plea of manslaughter accepted by the prosecution. Here is a tale of teenage gang violence in the inner cities which could have come straight from today's newspapers. It happened less than a decade after the end of the First World War.

The last case mentioned above has a very topical feel to it. 'Gangs' and 'feral' children and youths are popular folk devils of modern Britain. Fears of juvenile knife crime often go hand in hand with talk of gangs and 'postcode wars'. Such things too, we are led to believe, are ugly manifestations of modern society. Once again, the memories of the past have become sanitized and unwelcome facts artfully erased from history. Gangs and postcode wars are also nothing new, being an accepted part of life in Britain's big cities fifty or sixty years ago. For those unfamiliar with the expression, 'postcode war', the idea is that young people in some parts of cities such as London and Birmingham are so fiercely territorial and violent that they cannot leave the area of their own postcode and visit neighbouring districts for fear of being attacked. Newspapers treat this too as yet another alarming symptom of the degenerate state of modern society, with feral youths running riot through the streets. Just fancy, these youngsters cannot visit houses only a mile or two from their own home, or they will face mindless savagery. That was most definitely not a feature of children's lives as the baby boomers were growing up. Except, of course, it was.

In 1966 a book was published which studied boys growing up in East London at that time. In *Adolescent Boys in East London*, Peter Wilmott drew heavily upon interviews with, and extracts from the diaries of, boys living in London's East End, specifically the Bethnal Green area. In one interview, a teenage boy discusses the difficulties of moving freely around the East End at that time:

We don't go up towards Brick Lane because they'd come down and jump on *us*. We don't start on them. Anyone who wants to come in our area, they can as long as they don't start on us. We don't even go over to Stepney, because if we went over there, one night they would come over here, and they've got so many more than we have got that we wouldn't have a chance.

Which sounds uncannily like the postcode wars that one hears about today. Brick Lane and Stepney are only half a mile or so from Bethnal Green and yet some of the boys interviewed were reluctant to travel that far from their own homes, in case it triggered a violent response from others.

The thesis that our society is in some way 'broken' and producing large numbers of disaffected youths who will prey on respectable people, terrorising and even killing them if they get in the way, is a popular and widely-accepted one. Many people believe that there is something uniquely rotten about our society and that it has a toxic effect on some of the children born into and brought up in it. Sometimes the Internet is blamed, at others the breakdown in stable family life, combined with slack and trendy educational techniques used in our useless schools. Others believe that immigration, the precipitous decline in church attendance or the use of drugs play a part. Whatever the cause, all are agreed that it never used to be like this when they and their parents were at school. It is a modern phenomenon which has only really taken hold in the last twenty or twenty-five years.

The idea of feral youths or even feral children is a captivating one. The term 'feral' is chosen because this is the condition of formerly domesticated and biddable animals who have returned to the wild and begun to live again by their teeth and claws. It conjures up a marvellous image of semi-human children who although they live in our midst, conduct themselves as though they were characters from *Lord of the Flies*, living on a remote desert island. It might help to make sense of this myth if we were to see how large numbers of children and young people were actually behaving in this country during the 1950s and 1960s and to see if there was any appreciable difference between the conduct of wild young people in those days, compared with now.

On 9 May 1956, the *Manchester Guardian*, forerunner of today's *Guardian*, contained an article by a schoolteacher and youth club leader, headed, 'Children in Gangs; The Bond of Secrecy that Holds the Initiate in Thrall'. There had been a lot of talk in the newspapers in previous weeks about the extent to which juvenile delinquency and violence in Britain was associated with membership of gangs and the thrust of this article was that belonging to gangs was enormously common among boys from a very early age. Now of course there are gangs and gangs. William Brown, from the *Just William* stories, might be said to be the leader of a gang known as, 'The Outlaws'. That sort of thing was all pretty harmless, although some of William's activities these days would probably be enough to see him and his friends branded as feral youths! The gangs about which there was such concern in the early summer of 1956 were a very different matter.

The article in the *Manchester Guardian* focused upon an aspect of the gangs to which many schoolchildren and teenagers belonged, which will ring a bell with readers today. It will be remembered that 10-year-old Damilola Taylor was stabbed to death in 2000 for refusing to join, or have any connection with, a gang of schoolboys in south London. The boys who killed him were aged just 12 and 13. In 1956, this sort of thing was a great worry and boys who refused to join gangs or tried to leave them, were also being threatened with violence, as were their relatives. The woman who wrote the piece described how on being released from approved schools, some gang members tried to 'go straight'. They were not allowed to escape from the influence of the gang though and, to quote the author of the article:

> Boys coming out of approved schools and Borstals and trying to go straight got beaten up and finally in despair rejoined the gang, and eventually were picked up by the police again. In court if asked by the magistrates what had made them take to crime again they were silent. It was said that certain members of the gang attended the trial seated where they could watch the prisoner's face, fastened behind their coat lapels were razor blades which were thumbed back so they could catch the wretched prisoner's eye.

It was also claimed that the grandmother of one gang member who tried to break away from the gang kept an axe by the front door, as she was so terrified of reprisals against her or other members of her family.

A few weeks before this article appeared, a group of chief constables had announced that three-quarters of all juvenile crime was committed by children working together in groups. Gang culture was seen as a serious and growing problem that year. In July, 16-year-old Patrick Corr had been convicted at the Old Bailey of having stabbed to death an 18-year-old member of a rival group of young men with whom he had had an altercation. It was the sudden eruption of mindless violence which frightened ordinary people. This was in the main a problem of the larger cities, although, as we shall see, it could just as easily began in seaside towns like Margate or Brighton. Here is a typical example of the kind of thing which happened the year following Patrick Corr's conviction for little or no reason when the gangs at that time were looking for trouble.

In September 1957 two young men were stabbed in the space of a few hours, one aged 20 and the other just 17. They were random victims of a gang of youths on the rampage that night. In smaller towns too, gang-related savagery was simmering below the surface. Littleborough is a peaceful town which lies at the foot of the Pennine Hills, 12 miles from Manchester. On the night of 24 November 1957 fighting broke out between two groups of youths in the town. A bystander, Douglas Henderson, was struck on the head by a bottle, which left him seriously injured with a fractured skull. A young man who went to his aid, 17-year-old Derek Uttley, was stabbed twice in the leg. He was also struck round the head with a length of rubber hose which was being wielded as a weapon. Bricks were thrown, one of which hit the conductress on a passing bus. The incident ended as abruptly as it had begun, rating only a few inches in the next day's papers. It was not anything out of the ordinary for the late 1950s.

It would tedious and unnecessary simply to list the stabbings, beatings and fights in which gangs of young men, women and children were involved in the late 1950s. Exactly the same picture would emerge if, instead of the 1950s, we looked at the 1930s or indeed 1830s. Groups of young people banding together to fight and cause fear and alarm to older citizens are a scourge which, like the poor, will always be with us. Every shocking news item today about feral youths or vicious and disaffected schoolchildren can be matched by one from the years when the baby boomers were growing up.

The gangs of the 1950s and 1960s consisted largely of teenagers, some still at school and others who had left school, as one could at that time, at the age of 15. There were younger members, often the brothers of gang members who found a thrill in a tagging along on their older brothers' adventures. Then, as now, there was sometimes the feeling among the older boys that it was necessary to initiate youngsters into the life on the streets that they would soon be expecting to participate in.

It is altogether possible that some readers will be sceptical about much of what has been written above. Surely, they may think, we would have heard of all this, if it was indeed true that knife crime and gang warfare were as common as the author is making out? Part of the explanation is that the history we read can only ever be a selection, not a complete portrait of every single event which happened over any given period. Of necessity, we are only able to consider a limited amount of data and try somehow to fashion it into a coherent narrative. In the present case, we know that the Second World War was a time of the greatest slaughter which the world has ever seen. It would be dramatically satisfying if, after such terrible violence, we had a quiet period with pleasant childhoods for all. Later on of course, we will have the Swinging Sixties and the drugs and political violence of the 1970s, but why not have a peaceful couple of decades separating the war from all this?

It is difficult to know how else to account for the strange mythic narrative which has grown up about the decades immediately following the end of the war. By any objective measure that we can devise, they were not a whit better for children than today and by many standards were a good deal worse. The notion that modern Britain is somehow a terrible place for children to grow up is very much a product of newspapers and television. Frightening people about the prospects of their children dying before them are guaranteed to catch the attention of parents, if nothing else! Before looking at one very awful way that such anxieties are created and promoted, I want to give one last example of gang violence, which suddenly dominated the newspaper headlines in the early 1960s and has now been lost to memory. We read a lot about gangs in our big cities today, on which the police crackdown from time to time. Could we though imagine that the situation with gangs of youths today would grow serious enough to warrant the use of the RAF against them?

In the 1950s, there were the flick-knife carrying Teddy Boys who fought among themselves or with others. A few years later, there were the so-called Mods and Rockers. These were, respectively, smartly-dressed young men, often on motor scooters, and leather-jacketed youths on motorbikes. The two rival groups fought each other on the streets of Britain in the early 1960s. Here is a piece from the *Manchester Guardian* for 25 July 1964:

> A police air lift has been planned to cope with disturbances by mods and rockers over the August bank holiday period. London police will provide a standby force who will be flown by RAF Transport Command to any coastal trouble spots. After talks between the Metropolitan Police Commissioner and chief constables from coastal areas, Mr Henry Brooke, the Home Secretary, yesterday gave his approval to the scheme, which has been worked out in conjunction with the RAF. The RAF has surveyed possible landing strips on the east and south coast within striking distance of coastal resorts.

Now *that's* tackling gang violence; calling in the RAF to help in the fight against them! The headline for this piece may be seen in Illustration 10.

The precautions being taken for the August Bank Holiday that year were the result of widespread disturbances on the south and east coast, at places such as Clacton in Essex and Margate in Kent. After some skirmishes in Clacton, the Whitsun weekend in May saw more serious disorder by youths who travelled to peaceful seaside towns, apparently with the sole aim of fighting each other. In Margate, hundreds of youths fought pitched battles on the beach and then surged into the town itself, smashing shop windows and starting fires. There were some stabbings and forty youngsters were arrested. When they appeared in court the following week, the magistrate took the opportunity to make a few remarks about 'sawdust Caesars'. As he spoke, more violence erupted in the streets outside the court, leading to two young men being stabbed. There was fighting in the Sussex seaside town of Brighton as well at Whitsun, followed by sporadic disorder when the gangs returned to London. On 17 June, a 21-year-old man called George Monk was stabbed to death in a brawl between Mods and Rockers at Grays in Essex. Those charged with his murder included a 16-year-old and a 17-year-old. Anybody who believes that gangs and knife crime are a new phenomenon would do well to research the baby boomer period a little.

Before ending this chapter, I want to look at gun crime, with reference to children and teenagers. It is almost the received wisdom today that the use of guns by ever younger offenders is on the rise. This is often linked to gang-related violence. Surely there must be some way of establishing if this is in fact true? Are children really becoming involved with firearms now in a way which would have been unheard of sixty years ago?

This is what I described earlier as an awful example of the way in which anxieties are manufactured by politicians and newspapers with a view to persuading us that the country is in a deplorable state compared with how it was in those first couple of decades following the end of the war. At the time of writing, the news media are full of reports about a supposed rise in gun crime in Britain, with particular reference to the number of children who have been arrested for carrying or using firearms. The BBC, for instance, reported in March 2015 that 'Children as young as 10 were among hundreds of youngsters held over suspected firearms offences between 2013 and January 2015'. Newspapers linked all this to 'gangs'. In April 2016, the Office for National Statistics reported that there had been a rise in 'firearms offences'.

Here surely is solid evidence that childhood has changed since the baby boomers were children. It would have been inconceivable sixty years ago for a 10-year-old to be handling firearms or for a girl of 13 to have shot somebody, both incidents which were covered by the alarming figures obtained from various police forces by means of freedom of information requests in 2016. If this does not show how modern childhood is going off the rails, then nothing will!

There is a good deal more going on here than meets the eye and the claim that 'children as young as 10' are being arrested for 'firearms offences' is horribly misleading. The truth is that the offences which are being cited here were all far more common in the 1950s than they are now. Once again, we are being led up the garden path and in a most interesting fashion. At the back of it all is once again that fatal image of the happy childhood of the baby boomers, so different from life today.

Could we simply look at the statistics for this to make up our minds? Perhaps trying to find out how many young people under the age of 18 were arrested or convicted for offences associated with firearms in 1956 and then comparing them with last year's figures, say? There must be an objective measure of how many children were involved in 'gun crime' then and now, one would have thought. We come now to another of those tricky points that were mentioned in the Introduction; the near-impossibility of just placing one set of figures next to another and seeing which is the larger. To see why this would be, we must look at how 'firearms offences' were treated in the baby boomer years. First, some modern figures. Roughly 7,000 firearms offences are recorded each year in Britain. This figure is without doubt far higher than it was in the 1950s or 1960s. In the year ending March 2015, 7,866 firearms offences were recorded in England and Wales. At first sight, this sounds horrifying, as though we are living in the Wild West. A close look at the statistics, though, is more reassuring and has a bearing on our examination of crime and disorder among young people in the post-war years.

'Firearms offences' covers a very broad spectrum, ranging from firing a machine gun during a terrorist attack to covering a stick with a plastic carrier bag and telling the cashier in a local off-licence that you have a gun pointing at him. For most of us, 'guns' means firearms which use explosive ammunition and are capable of killing somebody. That is certainly the definition used by the Crown Prosecution Service and, before that, by the Director of Public Prosecutions. Only a minority of the 7,866 'firearms offences' recorded in England and Wales in the year ending 2015 involved proper guns of this sort. In the main, they were associated with replica weapons, airguns and claims by somebody to be carrying a firearm, even if this was impossible to verify. Interestingly, despite the public hysteria over gun crime, only nineteen people were actually killed by guns that year, the lowest figure since records began in this form in 1969. Fewer people are currently being killed each year by guns than during the 1960s.

The case of the 13-year-old girl who 'shot' somebody, according to the figures released in 2016, is particularly interesting as an example of the way that a fear can be worked up from almost nothing. In this case, not even an airgun was used. This child had fired an American BB gun, which projects miniature ball bearing by means of a spring-powered action. A BB gun might sting a little if you're hit by the ball from one, but they are little more than toys. If figures for 'firearms offences' had been collected and categorised in this way during the 1950s, with every child firing an air rifle or BB gun in public being classified as a dangerous criminal, then it is a fair guess that the statistics would have gone off the scale!

The connection between these statistics and life for the baby boomers as they were growing up is simple. Then, as now, airguns accounted for a huge proportion of firearms offences. These days, it is all but unheard for a child to have in his or her possession an air rifle or air pistol. No shop would dream of selling such a thing to a child and there can be few parents who would even think of giving an airgun to their children as a present, at least unless it was only to be used under the strictest of parental supervision. How very different the situation was sixty years ago. Illustration 5 shows an advertisement for airguns from the 1950s in which it is suggested that a rifle of this sort would make the ideal present for a child. How old is the boy in this advertisement; 11 or 12? Illustration 8 is from the Webley catalogue from the same period. At the bottom of the page, we can see a group of young boys playing with a pistol. There appears to be no adult in sight and the boys cannot be more than 11 or so.

Because they are not commonly seen in public now, a word or two about the nature of airguns might be timely. What one might call 'real' guns use a small explosive charge to propel a bullet, made of lead and sometimes jacketed with a harder metal, down the barrel. Airguns use compressed air to achieve the same end, which means that the little lead pellets leave the barrel with considerably less velocity than is the case with a genuine firearm. This does not mean, despite the claim in the advertisement in Illustration 5, that they are somehow 'harmless'; far from it. At close range, the pellets can penetrate the skin and need to be removed surgically and at a much greater range are capable of blinding somebody if they hit an eye. Hundreds of children under the age of 16 were blinded in one eye each year during the 1950s and 1960s and airguns were the main culprit.

It is not that 'firearm offences' are more prevalent now than they were a few years ago – there were almost certainly more airguns being discharged at people in 1959 than there are today – but rather that we take the misuse of these weapons more seriously today than we once did. For the baby boomers, shooting somebody in the face with an air rifle and blinding them in one eye was simply not a big deal. Even the courts treated such incidents as trifling mishaps. One or two real life cases might make this a little clearer.

On a Sunday afternoon in April 1950, two 16-year-old boys were walking along the banks of the canal running through the town of Bilston, on the outskirts of Wolverhampton. One of them felt a sharp pain in his back and when he turned round, he saw three boys: two were 13 and the other 12. All of them were carrying air rifles. Not unnaturally annoyed by being shot at, the two older boys gave chase and a running battle developed, with them firing catapults at the youngsters, who returned fire with their airguns. Eventually, the three boys with the rifles reached a low wall, which they crouched behind as they fired at the 16-year-olds. The youth who had been hit in the back was now hit again in the stomach. The other young man was less fortunate. He was shot in the face and spent five weeks in hospital. He was permanently blinded in one eye.

If something of this kind happened today, it would be viewed in a very dim light and those responsible would almost certainly be charged with GBH and, in addition to finding their way into the firearms-related crime figures, would in all likelihood sent to a young offenders' institution. As it was, the police confiscated the rifles and issued each of the three schoolboys with a summons for carrying the guns without a licence and also discharging a missile and causing injury. It was when the case reached Bilston magistrates court that the very great difference in attitude to gun-toting children in 1950 and today was revealed. The three boys were fined four shillings (20p) each on the first charge and two were fined £2 and the other £1 on the charge of firing a missile and causing injury. Having treated them with astonishing leniency, the magistrate then ordered that the police return their air rifles to them, warning that they should only be used in future in their back gardens.

There were few boys in the 1950s who did not at some stage handle or use an airgun. They circulated freely, with nobody taking much notice of them, as long as people were not badly injured. Boys lent them to their friends, sold them, swapped them for model yachts, tinkered with them to increase the muzzle velocity, drilled the front of pellets out to make dum-dum bullets and generally treated them as a natural accompaniment to normal boyhood. As the piece from the Internet quoted in Chapter 1 said, 'We were given air guns and catapults for our tenth birthdays'. Airguns were all over the place in those days.

The problem of airguns being widely carried and frequently used by children and young people grew steadily worse over the next ten years or so after the incident at Bilston. In February 1959 the police in the northern town of Oldham were growing tired of the number of children carrying and firing airguns on the streets. It was decided to make an example of one of these boys, a 13-year-old who was seen by the police firing an airgun in public. He was summoned to appear at the Juvenile Court, where he was fined £2 for firing his rifle in the street. Deputy Chief Constable John Kerin gave a statement after the boy's conviction, saying that the case had been brought to draw attention to 'the large number of boys between 10 and 15 having air rifles and ammunition in the street'.

In the next chapter we shall look a little more at the use of airguns by the baby boomer children. If 'firearms offences' had been pursued with as much vigour as they are today and properly collated statistics kept in the 1950s as they are today, there can be little doubt that the number of people injured by being shot at would be far higher than today. As for criminal damage caused by airguns, which makes up a large chunk of the modern figures for what we now refer to as 'gun crime', this was endemic. Shooting out streetlights, firing at passing cars or pedestrians, these things were part of the background of life at the time, especially in rougher neighbourhoods.

The closer we look at the world of baby boomer childhood, the more nearly it resembles the way of life of children and youths today. We see the same hooliganism, fears of gangs, knife culture, gun crime and so on. To be fair to the baby boomers, much the same picture would emerge from a close examination of any period in British history. The particular folk devils who give concern to respectable people might change in name, but the essential order of things remains the same. Whether we call them 'hooligans', as was done in the late nineteenth century, 'juvenile delinquents', which is what they were known as in the 1950s, or today's 'disaffected youth' or 'feral children', the phenomenon is the same. In each generation, a fair proportion of children and young people run riot, committing crimes which range up to and include murder. Always, the fear is the same, that this is some terrible contagion which is spreading and threatens to engulf civilized society.

It is to be suspected that not a few baby boomers, as well as those who have swallowed their fairy tales, will be shaking their heads at this point and while conceding that there might have been a few tearaways around, even sixty years ago, will insist that the great majority of children at that time were just high spirited and perhaps given to occasional bouts of mischievous behaviour. Most children did not associate with gangs or use knives against each other, they will say, being more likely to play out with their friends or go trainspotting. This brings us neatly to the subject of our next chapter, which will focus upon what 'playing out' actually meant for children growing up in the 1950s and 1960s. Articles in newspapers about childhood in the post-war years are almost invariably accompanied by black-and-white photographs of children trainspotting on a station platform or playing Cowboys and Indians. The overall impression given is that childhood was a much better time in those days, with innocuous hobbies and healthy, outdoor games. This is very misleading.

The truth is that many of the baby boomer children were running wild when they were 'playing out'; they were at least as likely to be throwing stones at trains or trying to derail them as they were to be carefully noting down their serial numbers in exercise books. Even toddlers were to be found trespassing on railway lines and accompanying their brothers and sisters when they engaged in bouts of vandalism. 'Feral' children and youths are nothing new. We shall be seeing a lot of this in the following chapter, which examines the practice of 'playing out'.

Chapter 4

Playing Out and Walking to School:
The Facts Behind the 'Freedom' Enjoyed by Young Baby Boomers

It is time now to look in detail at one or two of the 'freedoms' which children born during the baby boomer years enjoyed and which have largely withered away, freedoms such as walking to school alone and playing outdoors without the presence of adults. Quotation marks have been used because in a later chapter we will be examining the extent to which these things can really be thought of as freedoms. Before looking closely at what activities like 'playing out' actually entailed, we might first ask ourselves why so many children at that time were permitted, even encouraged, to vanish from adult oversight for many hours at a time, at a very early age. We have seen some of the hazards which attended the practice of 'playing out' or walking to and from school, and pretty grim reading they make too. Almost a thousand deaths a year from children knocked down by cars and many thousands of injuries from the same cause, many of them serious. A large number of girls were the victims of sexual abuse because they were out and about by themselves at a very young age, this abuse ranging all the way from indecent exposure up to rape and murder. We shall see in this chapter the dreadful injuries caused by the use and misuse of playground equipment. Fractured skulls, broken arms and teeth, even death, resulting from small children commonly being sent off in the care of older brothers and sisters; children who might themselves only be 11 or 12 years old.

One is forced to ask, whatever possessed mothers and father to allow their children to be placed in such dangerous situations? Were they blind to the hazards or did parents in those days simply not care as much about their offspring as we do today? In a previous chapter we read of Martin Brown, a four-year-old boy going to the local shop alone in 1968, who was abducted and killed on his way home. We saw also a six-year-old girl who was sent to school by herself and was, as a consequence, snatched from the street and murdered. Surely, common sense would tell us that four, five and six-year-olds cannot safely be permitted to wander the streets alone and that at the very least, they are liable to be knocked down while crossing the road? We know very well that allowing children of that age out on their own or even in the charge of their 11-year-old brothers or sisters, is not a brilliant idea. Robert Elms, mentioned in Chapter 1, tells us that by the age of nine or ten, it became common for him to be allowed to travel alone into central London by public transport and wander around all day. There can be very few mothers today who would think this a good idea and yet it was common enough fifty years ago. Is there a single mother today who would give her nine-year-old child a travel pass and send him off to explore central London by himself? Why didn't parents in the 1950s and 1960s see how undesirable these things were?

To understand the whole concept of 'playing out' and sending children off for the day with instructions no to come back until teatime, a state of affairs which generates so many wonderful memories in older British adults, we have to put ourselves in the position of parents in the early 1950s, the beginning of the baby boomer heyday of playing out and childhood independence. Although, in retrospect, those who were children at the time talk of the marvellous freedom which they enjoyed, the truth is that they really had little choice at all in the matter: they were very often forced to spend a lot of their time outside the home without any adults to take care of them. This puts rather a different slant on the childhood 'freedom' of which such a fetish is now made. It was not so much that they particularly wished to roam the streets all day, but that their mothers often sent them out of the house in the morning and told them not to return until teatime. Even when they were not actually sent from the house in this way, there was so little to do at home in those days, that walking the streets was often preferable to remaining cooped up indoors.

One point which needs to be borne in mind when thinking about childhood for the baby boomers, particularly in the early years of the period, that is to say the 1950s, is that mothers at that time were almost invariably synonymous with housewives. Few went out to work. They were tied to the home and both caring for this and looking after the children took a great deal of hard work. Not only did homes lack most of the domestic gadgets and facilities which we now take for granted such as washing machines or even hot water on tap, but standards of cleanliness were also in general much higher than they are now. Being a housewife for most mothers meant ensuring that not only the house was spotless, but that the outside of their home and, in cities, even the nearby pavement was also clean and tidy. Behaviour of this sort would these days be seen as verging on the obsessive. In working-class city streets though, it was very much the rule that all the women would clean the front doorstep and window sills once a week with a block of abrasive, synthetic stone called donkeystone, all at the same time, and then wash down the pavement as well. All of which, along with the many other chores, took time; a lot of time. The average mother in the early 1950s spent an astonishing eleven hours a day working at home. Illustration 9 shows housewives in the 1950s donkeystoning their front steps.

There were implications for children in this frantic, never-ending round of domestic drudgery. It was not easy to get on with the chores with small children underfoot. A family with three children would mean the mother making twenty-eight beds a week, to give but one example. These days we have duvets which can simply be smoothed down in a few seconds, but sixty years ago, sheets, blankets and counterpanes were the order of the day. This daily chore alone was a tiring and time-consuming one. Almost all homes were heated by coal at the beginning of the 1950s and one of the first tasks for any housewife on rising would, from September to April, be to rake out the ashes of the previous day's fire and carefully build a new one in the fireplace. Even in the summer, many homes would need a coal fire to be built, so that the family had hot water. With no supermarkets, a shopping trip each day on foot was necessary. The lack of a refrigerator meant that only enough food for that day was usually purchased.

Some days were entirely taken up with domestic work to the exclusion of all else. Monday was washday in the 1950s and 1960s. There was no question at that time of popping a load in the washing machine and getting on with something else. In 1950, fewer than 5 per cent of households had a washing machine and doing the wash was a major operation, involving boiling up copious quantities of hot water and filling a copper. It was backbreaking work, because all the clothes then needed to be scrubbed by hand on a washboard, rinsed several times and then put through a hand-operated mangle. Not only clothes, but also sheets and towels had to be laboriously washed by hand. It was hard work which would have tired out an able-bodied man. If it was raining, then clothes would need to be dried indoors, in front of the fire, draped on clothes horses or even hung from the picture rail. Doing all this with children running about would be impossible. If the clothes horse, laden with clean shirts, were to be accidentally knocked into the fireplace, everything on it would need to be washed again.

On school days, mothers had a clear run at things like washday, but during the school holidays and at weekends, it was a different matter. Some way had to be devised of keeping the children out of the way, so that the housework could be done. In a world bursting with electronic entertainment such as televisions, tablets, games consoles, mobile telephones and all the other paraphernalia of modern childhood, it is hard to imagine how empty and bleak most homes were sixty years ago. After all, the average home in Britain now boasts no fewer than five colour televisions; in 1950, perhaps one home in ten had just a single black-and-white set. There was only one channel and programmes were not broadcast during the day. There really was nothing much to entertain or occupy children. Of course, most homes had a radio, but the only children's programme during the daytime was *Listen with Mother*. Many homes would have a few books, board games and toys, maybe a piano. There were hardly any record players. In short, there was nothing at all for children to do indoors when their mother was too busy to give them her undivided attention. The obvious, indeed for many the only, solution was to shoo the children out of the house in the morning and tell them to stay out until teatime. Sometimes, as Robert Elms says, a Red Rover daily bus pass might be bought for the child if the family lived in London, but this would be an exceptional treat. Mostly, the children would be expected to find their friends and then amuse themselves in any way they saw fit.

Even if one's mother did not actually chuck one out of the house so that she could get on with things, there was little incentive to stay indoors. Only those who grew up during this period can have any conception of just how dreary and grey life could be in those far-off times. In the autumn and winter only one room in the house would typically be heated. This meant that if a child wished to stay warm, he or she would be compelled to stay in that room. There was little to do indoors and even if their mothers did not want them out of the way so that they could get on with things, many children saw leaving the house and drifting about the streets, parks or fields as preferable to being cooped up in the house with nothing to do. We looked in some detail at the murder of Iris Dawkins in Southampton in 1960 and readers are reminded that this took place on a chilly, damp Saturday afternoon in February. She and her friends were playing Cowboys and Indians in the local park because there was simply nothing else for a group of children to do in those days.

Quite apart from the idea of a parent allowing a child of nine to go off and play in a park without any adults around, we need to ask ourselves what would motivate children themselves to hang round a cold park all afternoon in that way. The answer is that there was absolutely nothing else *to* do. No inviting indoor shopping malls to visit, no money to spend, nothing to do at home and nothing else to do outdoors, other than play in a park in winter. In many ways, this was a pretty grim world for ordinary children, who had to entertain themselves as best they could.

One feature of the baby boomer years which has come to be seen as part of a desirable lifestyle for children is of course walking to school, instead of being driven there by a parent. As we have seen, children walked to school alone from a very early age up until the 1970s. In 1971, 80 per cent of seven and eight-year-olds were still walking to school by themselves. The reason for this dangerous custom is pretty much the same as that responsible for the popularity of 'playing out'.

According to the National Travel Survey in 2013, the average primary school pupil now lives 1.6 miles from his or her school. We do not have comparable and accurate figures for the 1950s, although it was probably a little less. Let us work with the present-day distance and consider the implications for taking a child to school on foot and then collecting him or her at home time in the afternoon. Each journey there and back to the school would be about three miles, which at a brisk walking pace, an adult may cover in an hour or so. This would mean that, walking at a reasonable pace, the two trips would take about two hours. Of course, for half that time, one will be walking with a young child, who might only be able to walk at about half an adult's speed. This will have the effect of doubling the journey time for half the total time spent walking to and from the school. Which in turn means that any parent wishing to escort a child to primary school in this way, must on average allow three hours a day in order to do so.

Incidentally, these figures show precisely why all current efforts to encourage primary school children to walk to school are doomed. They mean either that parents will have to spend an extra fifteen hours a week walking or that children under the age of 11 will be sent off by themselves each morning, with all the unfortunate side-effects of increased injury and death from road accidents which this would inevitably entail. Neither is likely. Sixty years ago, the prospect of taking three hours each weekday from the frantically busy schedule of the average mother and housewife was unthinkable. It was not an ideal solution, but allowing small children to walk to school either alone or being looked after by an older brother or sister seemed to most parents the only sensible option. Few people would wish to see a return to those days.

Entrusting very small children to the care of their older siblings was a very common custom as the baby boomers grew up. They were often used as escorts to take younger siblings to school in the morning. If there were no older brothers or sisters around then, at a pinch, four-, five- and six-year-olds would be sent to school alone or on errands to local shops, but if a 10-year-old brother or sister could be dragooned into helping, that was preferable. The sight of children who were barely out of nappies trotting around after nine-year-olds who had been given the job of taking care of them was not an unusual one. This may have been marginally better than leaving the smaller children to fend for themselves when they were out and about, but it was hardly ideal. It was not until the mid-1970s that objective and clinical data came to light which perfectly illustrated one of the particular dangers produced by this practice.

In the early 1970s a doctor called Cynthia Illingworth was working at the Sheffield Children's Hospital. She began to be concerned about the dreadful injuries suffered by young children attending the hospital, injuries which she said were comparable to those seen in the victims of severe road accidents. Severed fingers, crushed limbs, shattered skulls, broken legs and eye injuries were among the most noticeable ones that Dr Illingworth encountered. The picture was pretty much the same at other hospitals across Britain at that time. The strange thing was that most doctors and nurses simply took this carnage for granted, seeing nothing at all out of the ordinary about the numbers of casualties among the under-11 age group. It had, after all, been like that for as long as anybody could remember.

One of the discoveries that Cynthia Illingworth made was that when children under the age of 11 lost the tips of their fingers, these would re-grow without any medical intervention. This is in itself curious; wherever did she find so many children with parts of fingers that had been cut off? It is, after all, an incredibly rare childhood injury today. The answer lies of course in the habit of playing out in playgrounds and parks. These days, you would probably not have much scope for investigating the re-growth of chopped-off children's fingers, but in the 1960s there were plenty to look at. Dr Illingworth wanted to know why that was.

Before looking at Cynthia Illingworth's findings, a word or two about playgrounds and parks might not come amiss, otherwise nobody under the age of forty will be likely to understand what follows. There were two factors in the accidents that Cynthia Illingworth investigated. The first of these was that the majority of the injuries seen were a result of accidents taking place during play, particularly in playgrounds. The second was that in most cases, the accidents had taken place when no adult had been present.

Modern British playgrounds are safe and inviting places, where few children come to harm. The equipment is, wherever possible, made of or covered with plastic, nylon or rubberized material and the surfaces beneath the roundabouts and swings are almost invariably soft and a little springy. Roundabouts have governors fitted to them which prevent them from travelling too fast and all moving objects present plastic surfaces in the direction in which they are travelling. In 1974, when Dr Illingworth was conducting her research, playgrounds were very different places. Much of the equipment had remained unchanged for almost the whole of the twentieth century and there was little plastic to be seen. The playgrounds and parks of the baby boomers were constructed of concrete, steel and wood.

These days, when children trip up in a playground, they are likely to land on a rubberised surface whose specific purpose is to soften the impact of a fall. Even a grazed knee is a rare occurrence. Until the 1970s, the ground in playgrounds was as likely as not to be an expanse of concrete.

Not just any old concrete, but that strange mix containing many pebbles and stones was a popular foundation for playground equipment in the years at which we are looking. Falling onto this from more than a couple of feet meant running the risk of a broken bone. Stumbling onto it with bare knees, which all children displayed then, often drew blood. This was a minor inconvenience compared with the results if a child landed head first on the concrete at high speed, something which was sure to happen to at least one child during an afternoon of playing in such an environment.

The equipment in children's play areas has changed out of all recognition since Cynthia Illingworth carried out her research. Illustration 3 shows a playground in the 1950s. The swing boats are no more, gone are the rocking horses – even the witch's hat has been consigned to the dustbin of history. These devices were seriously dangerous. Take the swing boat, which consisted of a quarter of a ton of steel and wood, suspended from a metal frame. Along the centre ran a wooden beam, with rungs attached to it. Some children sat on this, while others hung on the side. Others pushed the massive structure back and forth, slowly at first, but with gathering speed and force. Sometimes, children ran in front of the moving swing boat and had teeth knocked out or broken. On other occasions, they would be struck on the head or arm and bones would break. Sometimes, smaller children would lose their grip and fall off. If they were not careful, the swing boat, with its cargo of children, would then swoop down and knock them over.

On the face of, the rocking horse was one of the gentler rides to be found in the playgrounds. A long, wooden box, with metal seats which one straddled and a crude metal representation of a horse's head at the front. One may be seen in Illustration 4. This was essentially something for the smaller children, half a dozen of whom could sit in a line on top of the rocking horse. The mechanism which was hidden beneath the base allowed the thing to move backwards and forward with a swinging and bouncing action. Once it was going, the rocking horse could move very quickly and there was always the chance that the child riding at the front would be hurled forward over the horse's head and onto the concrete. One recalls Cynthia Illingworth's shrewd observation in her 1975 report on playground injuries: 'The younger children were at particular risk on equipment such as the wooden rocking horse or roundabout, when the speed of operation could be controlled by older children.'

The playground environment and equipment was hazardous enough in itself, but this could have been ameliorated by the presence of responsible adults, ready to step in and call a halt to especially reckless actions on the part of the older children. Unfortunately, many of the very small children were being looked after only by siblings who were themselves of primary school age, that is to say 11 or under. It was a recipe for disaster. If the rocking horse were pushed to its limit, it was very difficult for the small children to hold on. Remember that there might well be three- and four-year-olds sitting on the rocking horse and there was a certain amount of competition on the part of the older children, especially the boys, to see who could make it buck the most.

A type of injury seen again and again in children at that time was crushed fingers and hands, which was how Dr Illingworth gained her data on severed fingertips. The chief culprit implicated here was that old favourite, the witch's hat. Imagine if you will a conical structure made from lengths of steel piping welded together into a rough imitation of a tall witch's hat. This contraption, about eight feet high, was placed over a stout metal pole planted in the concrete. It was fixed to the pole at the top by a universal joint which allowed it to swing back and forth and rotate freely. Children clung onto the skeleton frame and kicked off with their feet, causing the 'hat' to move crazily around the pole. As it did so, the heavy steel construction banged hard against the metal pole from which it was suspended, crushing the hand, and occasionally severing the fingertips, of any child hanging onto that side.

Because the frenetic activity of the playground was led by children, there was little restraint or common sense to be found. An older child might rock the wooden horse back and forth with increasing violence until a child was hurled off onto the concrete, sometimes breaking an arm or fracturing his or her skull. The same thing happened on the roundabouts, which could reach very high speeds. This resulted in four-year-olds being thrown head first onto a concrete surface at 30 miles an hour. Little wonder that some of the injuries seen in British hospitals at that time among children who had been playing in the local park resembled road traffic accidents!

Those who were at school during this period will know that the sight of a child with his or her arm or leg in plaster was a common one. It was a ritual to get all one's classmates to sign the cast. Today, it is very rare to see a child struggling to school on crutches with a leg in plaster up to the knee. Playgrounds, and life generally, is a lot less risky for children compared with half a century or more ago.

Once again, many older people are sentimental about this awful state of affairs, denouncing efforts to create a safer play environment for children as being symptomatic of the 'Nanny State'. They reminisce about the swing boats and witch's hats, bemoaning their loss, while quite forgetting the havoc they wreaked and the misery which was caused to the victims of such dangerous pieces of playground equipment. Gradually though, over the course of a few decades, soft surfaces replaced the concrete and the more dangerous equipment was quietly pensioned off. Playgrounds today are infinitely safer and more welcoming places for children than once they were. These improvements, combined with the fact that one seldom or never sees gangs of 10-year-olds ruling the roost in playgrounds these days and regulating the speed of the roundabouts and swings on which very young children are riding, means that casualty departments are no longer crowded with five-year-olds with broken arms, crushed hands and feet, missing fingers or fractured skulls.

Of course, the injuries sustained in the course of a visit to the local park did not all result from unsafe swings, slides and so on. When children are playing without any adult oversight or supervision, they are perfectly capable of creating mayhem, even in the safest and least threatening of environments. Before looking at other hazards to be found in playgrounds and parks, we pause to consider once again the statement quoted in the Introduction, from Steve Stack's book, *21st Century Dodos*: 'We should allow our children to play in the streets, climb trees, walk to school, play down the park, cycle round the neighbourhood, go to the corner shop, etc. They will become better adults as a result.' Let's think a little more about, 'playing down the park' and what this might have entailed for baby boomers as they grew up.

When looking with a jaundiced eye at the leisure activities of modern children, the one thing which always crops up is playing Cowboys and Indians. It epitomizes what many older people feel was right about their own childhoods and contrasts favourably with all that they see as wrong about what they think they know about childhood today. Sexting! Cyberbullying! Accessing online pornography! Honestly, the things that kids get up to these days! Why, when we were their age, we were playing Cowboys and Indians in the local park. Happier, healthier and more carefree times, or so we are supposed to believe.

The image that most of us have of children playing Cowboys and Indians is of cheeky little fellows pointing their fingers, while shouting, 'Bang, bang, you're dead!' Perhaps they had a toy pistol firing harmless caps, but that was about the most dangerous thing one might see in a game of that sort. In the last chapter, we learned of little Iris Dawkins, who was stabbed to death and her body ferociously mutilated in the aftermath of a game of Cowboys and Indians played in the local park. Such deaths were then, as they are now, very rare. Other injuries resulting from the playing Cowboys and Indians were not. In fact they were appallingly common and included children regularly losing eyes, as well as being stabbed and beaten.

One of the things which baby boomers tend to forget when enthusing about the happy days when children went out by themselves, without their parents, and whiled away the hours by playing Cowboys and Indians, is that in all too many cases, these games were played not with toys, but with real knives, real guns and real bows and arrows. This led, unsurprisingly, to the most shocking harm being inflicted on some of the participants of such games, including the blinding in one eye each year of somewhere in the region of 300 children.

In the early 1960s, a British hospital analysed every case of eye injuries suffered by children over the course of the ten years up to 1960 and leading to the child being treated in their hospital; in other words, for the whole of the 1950s. The Wolverhampton Eye Infirmary, which reported its findings in the *Lancet* in December 1962, under the heading of 'Some common causes of eye injury in the young', discovered that 610 children over that period had needed to be admitted to their establishment for trauma to their eyes. When looked at closely, something disturbing emerged, which was that the great majority of the injuries arose not from accidents but rather from deliberate assaults by other children. These ranged from airguns being fired and arrows shot from bows to knife wounds and things such as marbles and stones being thrown or catapulted at children's faces. Much of this took place while games of Cowboys and Indians were being played. In the course of mimic warfare, children as young as 10 would wave penknives around or fire air rifles at their opponents, with devastating effect. Bows and arrows were also implicated in many eye injuries.

A word might not come amiss here about bows and arrows. It is rare these days to see children playing with bows and arrows which, when they *are* seen, are invariably flimsy plastic things with arrows tipped with rubber suckers. Bows and arrows for the baby boomers tended to be a lot more robust and dangerous. A popular type consisted of a steel rod covered with black plastic tubes and bent to accommodate the string. These were sold in toy shops and were capable of propelling arrows with considerable force. The arrows themselves were tipped either with brass points or suckers. The suckers, though, were easily removed and the tip of the arrow sharpened with a penknife, which left the child with a deadly weapon, quite capable of taking out somebody's eye.

Doctors in casualty departments in the late 1950s believed that there was a direct and strong link between the popularity of television programmes such as *Robin Hood* and *Davy Crockett* and the number of injuries to eyes caused by arrows. Something should be said about the Davy Crockett craze which swept the country during the 1950s. In 1954 and 1955, the American television channel ABC produced a mini-series about the life of Western frontiersman Davy Crockett. There were five episodes, each lasting an hour. Davy Crockett became a cult, both in America and Britain, with sales of imitation coonskin hats, which the hero wore, reaching astronomical levels. There cannot be a child who grew up in the 1950s who will not at once be able to sing along with the show's signature song. 'Davy, Daaavy Crockett, King of the wild frontier . . .'! All of which sounds marvellously redolent of another era and will bring back memories for baby boomers of the days that they didn't need to look at a lot of sex and violence on the Internet, but were able to play thrilling outdoor games, as they re-enacted the life story of Davy Crockett.

In the 1950s, for those whose parents could not afford to buy them a bow and arrow from the local toyshop, there was a free alternative, which was to make one's own. This is an art which was widely practiced sixty years ago, but is now unknown. One needs a slim and springy straight shoot of a bush; hazel is perfect. It is simply necessary to cut this shoot off about four feet in length and then make notches in the end. Bending it and attaching twine to the ends will give you a most serviceable, if not particularly accurate, bow. All that is then needed is to cut and sharpen some arrows and you are ready to go. One can achieve precisely the same effect with garden canes; bamboo is very bendy and makes a great bow.

That playing with real bows and sharp arrows was once nothing at all out of the ordinary may be seen from a children's book written a little earlier than the baby boomer years in 1930. *Swallows and Amazons*, by Arthur Ransome, tells the story of children sailing and having various adventures in the Lake District, ten years before the start of the Second World War. The children in this book are left largely to their own devices as they play around on the water and fire arrows at each other, using home-made bows of the sort described above. When a film was made of the book in 1973, arrows were shown being fired with very little care for Health and Safety. At that time, the idea of children using bows and arrows which were capable of injuring others was still not outlandish. These days though, when the film is shown on television, the scenes involving arrows thudding into woodwork near a child's head are edited out.

The account of the findings from the Wolverhampton Eye Infirmary, just one hospital in an average British city, make chilling reading. 'The greatest number of injuries were caused by missiles, assaults and arrows', 'the commonest cause of blind eyes were arrows, airguns and assaults'. The Registrar at the hospital made some comments which indicated his own views on children playing Cowboys and Indians. Blaming lack of parental supervision for many of the injuries seen at the hospital, he remarked that children needed instruction, full-time supervision and training while they were growing up. Obviously, he was not a believer in the virtues of their playing Cowboys and Indians in the local park without any adults about to watch over them! He also suggested that it would be a good idea if the sale of airguns, bows and arrows and catapults could be banned to those under the age of 14, which indicated that many shops were at that time selling such potentially lethal weapons to younger children.

Bows and arrows were not the only 'real' weapons used when playing games of Cowboys and Indians. Penknives were often used in play fights, sometimes with the natural consequence that somebody ended up getting stabbed. Guns too, specifically airguns, were a regular accompaniment of such games, with awful consequences. In May 1956, a number of surgeons signed their names to a letter sent to the *British Medical Journal*. They were drawing attention to what they saw as the irresponsible nature of the Davy Crockett films which were then being shown on British television. The surgeons claimed that eye injuries among children had risen dramatically since the screening of the programmes which had caused children to play Cowboys and Indians with even more enthusiasm than usual. One surgeon, Mr Dykes Bower, said that there was always at least one child in his own hospital with an eye injury, having fallen victim to this new craze.

What are known technically as 'penetrating injuries' to the eye are now very rarely seen in children, so-called 'blunt trauma' being far more commonly recorded. The decline in use of bows and arrows, catapults and airguns by children has been responsible for this trend. A study in Scotland some years ago found that penetrating injuries to the eye were now almost unknown when children turned up at A&E. In the course of a year, only one child in the whole of Scotland lost the sight of an eye and this was due simply to tripping up at home, rather than being assaulted. A child losing an eye from an arrow wound would probably be headline news in today's Britain, rather than the run-of-the-mill affair it once was.

Reading the report published about the Wolverhampton research sheds a good deal of light on the reality of playing out in 1950s Britain from people who were in an excellent position to know just what children were getting up to when they were out and about without their parents. The 6–10 age group suffered the most injuries from having things thrown at them. As the registrar explained, if there was nobody of his own age to throw stones or marbles at, 'then a helpless younger child is often a convenient target'. Writing in the *Manchester Guardian* on 1 May 1963 about the Wolverhampton findings, Betty Jerman observed: 'How few of the accidents are due to the cheerful rioting of children at play. Instead one has a picture of children with lethal weapons in their hands and no understanding of the menace which can bring tragedy to a playmate.' This

... road sign from the 1950s; note the young schoolchildren confidently crossing the road
... e on their way to school.

2. Boys trainspotting at a railway station; other children were sabotaging and attempting to derail trains at this time.

3. A playground in 1950s Britain; the presence of adults was often the only thing holding dangerous behaviour in check.

The playground rocking horse, cause of many serious injuries.

An open penknife. Such knives were almost universally carried by baby boomer boys.

6. A 1957 advertisement for air rifles, encouraging fathers to equip their young sons with such weapons.

7. An air pistol in the Webley catalogue. Note the age of the boys firing a pistol unsupervised at the bottom of the page.

A souvenir from the seaside.
...ives were a ubiquitous
...companiment to baby
...omer boyhood.

Housewives cleaning their
...nt steps in the 1950s.
...usework took up the entire
..., leaving little time for
...ying with children.

Boy, 11, accused of murder

Girl "victim of frenzied attack"

Police air lift to beat seaside riots

10. Newspaper headlines from 1960 and 1964; a child who murdered a little girl and rioting youths whom the RAF was called in to help control.

11. Children playing on a bomb site in the 1950s, something about which many older people have happy memories.

Little wonder that more children were admitted to hospital for accidental injuries sixty years
o! Children on a bomb site fool around with a pickaxe.

A surviving bomb site in London. Attractive to children as they were, they were hardly safe
desirable places for children to play.

14. An iron lung. Some children spent the rest of lives in such contraptions after contracting polio in the 1940s and 1950s.

15. A ward full of children in iron lungs. There were a thousand of these machines operating Britain in the 1950s.

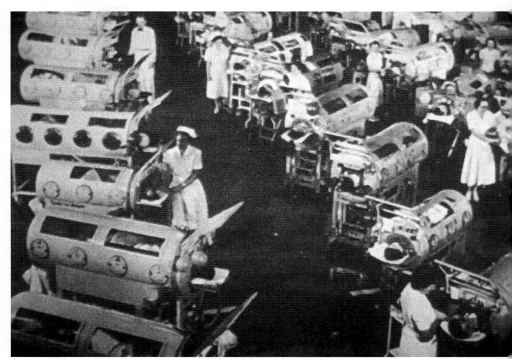

is not, to say the least of it, the image most of us have about children 'playing out' in the baby boomer years!

A regular feature in newspapers each autumn is the claim that some school or other has either banned the playing of conkers or imposed stringent safety measures, requiring, for instance, that those playing conkers should wear protective goggles. Just as regularly, one may rely upon elderly baby boomers to write to the papers, complaining of either the 'Nanny State' or 'Health and Safety gone mad'. It is interesting in this context to see conkers being specifically listed in the report in the *Lancet* in 1962 as being among the missiles which had caused children to be admitted to hospital with lacerations and bruising to their eyes. Perhaps a little more 'Health and Safety' might not have come amiss fifty years ago!

Of course, fighting games such as Cowboys and Indians or the even more popular one of Germans and English, re-fighting the recently-ended war, did not take place just in parks. Bomb sites were the almost exclusive domain of children in the first ten or fifteen years after the Second World War and they provided a valuable space where all manner of wild and undisciplined play could take place. There are very few bomb sites left and so the expression might need a little explanation.

The bombing by the German air force of many British cities led to the destruction of a lot of houses and other buildings. Some of these were so badly damaged that nobody bothered to repair them and they were left standing empty for years. Sometimes, the unsafe buildings would be demolished and just an expanse of bricks and rubble would be left. So you would have a half-ruined house surrounded by a rubble-strewn wilderness.

Children had great fun on bomb sites. Old pieces of glass could be shattered, bits of rusty metal hurled, bricks thrown at each other and fires started. Adults, glad that the streets were not being taken over by 'feral' children and youths, were only too happy to leave the youngsters to their own devices on the bomb sites. At least while they were on the rampage there, they weren't smashing windows in people's homes or starting fires where they could do any real harm. The only ones who were harmed by the fighting and destruction were the children themselves.

In Illustrations 11 and 12, we can see children playing on a London bomb site. There is a decided lack of Health and Safety to be observed in these pictures. Just look at the boy with the pickaxe! And what about the fire that is burning in the other photograph? These pictures show exactly what bomb sites were like in the years following the end of the Second World War. They were enormously attractive places to children, for the simple reason that no grown-ups interfered with what was going on when they saw children playing there. There was little harm that they could do to anybody's property and it was felt that they might as well let off steam in such places as anywhere else.

There are very few bomb sites left today, but one was tracked down for this book! Illustration 13 shows perhaps the last remaining bomb site in London, which is to be found in Noble Street, near London Wall. Its survival is due to a curious trick of fate. When the *Luftwaffe* was pounding Britain in the early 1940s, many buildings in central London were destroyed by the bombing. Occasionally, the destruction wrought in this way revealed things which had been hidden from view for centuries or even millennia. When a row of Victorian buildings in Nobel Street was demolished by a bomb, it was found that it had been erected on the remains of a Roman fort. Once the rubble was cleared away, the site was left unmolested, so that the base of the Roman wall was visible. Nothing else was done and so a Second World War bomb site has, in effect, been permanently preserved.

Looking down at the bomb site in Noble Street it is, even many years later, possible to see the attraction of such locations for children who had nothing else to do. What might be found if we were to dig down a little? Treasure? Would it be possible to climb up those walls, by hanging onto the ivy growing there? There is something wild and untamed about spots like this. They are quite different from the neat and regulated parts which make up the rest of the city, a patch of wildness and romance, an escape from the real, mundane world.

We have looked at some of the dangers of playing out, things which killed hundreds of children and led to 300 losing eyes each year, to say nothing of all those fractured skulls, lost fingers and broken arms and legs. What else did the baby boomers get up to when there were no adults around to keep an eye on things? The railway was one perennial source of entertainment, both for the hobby of trainspotting, as well as other less desirable occupations. Trespassing on railway lines and the surrounding land was something of an institution among the baby boomers; hence the films made which warned against the practice. The thundering steam trains exercised a terrible fascination for children, which led to a number of deaths and presented something of a problem for the authorities. Trainspotters could be a nuisance, but were in the main a fairly law-abiding bunch. Any newspaper article about 1950s childhood is almost certain to include a photograph of a group of boys standing on a platform with notebooks in their hands. Such a scene is shown in Illustration 2. A sharp contrast, we are invited to believe, with the kind of things modern boys of that age might get up to. Except of course, children were just as prone to dangerous mischief then as they are now.

In May 1959, the management of British Railways appealed to parents and teachers to warn children about the danger of attacking and trying to derail trains. In the northern county of Lancashire, the situation had become particularly grave. There has been many incidents of stones and bottles thrown at passing trains, which smashed windows and had injured a driver and passengers, but this was nothing compared to what had happened at Orrell, near Wigan. Heavy beams of wood had been laid across the line there, with the evident intention of derailing a train, and the line had had to be closed for a time. At Bolton, points had been jammed with stones, while at Eccles an oil drum had been rolled down an embankment and onto the line. At Manchester's Victoria Station, somebody had released the brakes on a stationery parcel van, causing it to roll into the sidings, where fortunately it hit the buffers. There was a very real fear that if this vandalism were not checked, then a serious train crash might be caused.

Four years later, the situation had deteriorated dramatically and on 30 May 1963, British Railways Divisional Superintendent Charles Steed called a press conference in Manchester to draw public attention to what was seen by some as a crisis. An engine driver, invited by the police to address the meeting, said that the points at Newton Heath were known among drivers as 'Sabotage Corner', due to the number of attacks on trains and attempts to derail them. All this was carried out by children. Quoting part of the statement read out by Inspector Steed will give some idea of what the engine drivers were having to put up with: 'Last year in this division we had 1,717 complaints of children trespassing on railway property and 569 complaints of stones and other missiles being thrown at trains. Every year children are killed and injured because they trespass on railway property. Some of them are young toddlers.' Thomas Hinley, the engine driver who talked about 'Sabotage Corner', revealed that his stoker had been knocked unconscious by a brick thrown into the cab by a child.

These dangerous actions by children were the dark side of the enthusiasm for steam engines and trainspotting which was such a well-known feature of 1950s boyhood. Once they had gained access to the tracks, some children would follow the harmless but dull hobby of trainspotting, while others would try and cause accidents. As usual, a number of these boys were burdened with much younger siblings, some of them, as Inspector Steed said, being only toddlers. The solution for the older boys was plain: they took the small children with them onto the land running alongside the railway line.

Various games would be played when trespassing on the railways. There was for example what we would now call an urban myth that a train could be derailed if a penny was laid on the rail. The experiment was conducted many times, without success. Another game, one which could easily lead to death, was called 'Last Across'. This was a forerunner of the modern game of 'Chicken'. A group of boys would engage to run across the tracks in front of an oncoming express train. The winner was the one who delayed longer than any of his playmates in crossing the tracks. It was not particularly uncommon for children to be killed by trains while playing this game, which accounts for all the posters and public information films produced at this time in an effort to discourage children from playing near the railway.

It was not only on the railways that vandalism was being carried out by children who were playing out. A couple of years before the attacks on trains in Manchester were getting out of hand, there had been trouble at Manchester Airport. On 9 May 1961, the police announced that they were stepping up patrols at the airport because engineers had reported that the landing lights which guided aeroplanes into the airport were being smashed in increasing numbers by stones and airguns. The police believed that children gathering to watch the planes landing and taking off were the culprits. Still in the vicinity of Manchester, there was more trouble with vandalism being caused with airguns in September of the same year. The Crompton district was plagued with youngsters shooting out the streetlights and the borough surveyor, Mr J. E. Gledhill, announced that he had posted lookouts with binoculars to try and identify the children who were behind the spate of attacks, the latest of which was in Buckstones Road.

In the same year that children were shooting out the lights on the runway of Manchester Airport, vandalism was a serious problem in other parts of the country. A council meeting at Ashton-under-Lyne on 12 April 1961 discussed recent damage caused to Stamford Park by children. This included breaking into the refreshment room and trashing it, digging up the putting green, sinking a boat and destroying swans' nests and smashing the eggs they contained. Alderman J. Booth, Chairman of the Parks Committee, said that, 'The 60 MPs who voted for the return of corporal punishment were right'. To which Councillor J. Eason responded that, 'It is the fathers who should be flogged. Some parents take absolutely no interest in their children.' The following month, the local council at Haydock, near Liverpool, announced that the parents of children found engaging in vandalism would be evicted from their council-owned homes. Lights had been smashed, garden walls pushed over and gates torn from their hinges. This sort of vandalism was caused by children 'playing out', that is to say, running riot without any adult supervision.

Returning to trouble caused by children on the railways, we note that on 16 March 1961, the same year that patrols were instituted to combat the shooting out with airguns of the lights at Manchester Airport, the driver of a train was shot by an air rifle. A freight train was passing through Rose Bridge, when the driver, Tom Abbotts of Wigan, felt a sharp pain to the side of his head. When he removed his cap, he found that there was a hole through it. Had the pellet hit him in the eye, then he would certainly have been blinded. Mr Abbotts said after the incident, 'I've had mattresses, tin cans and even iron bedsteads flung at my engine, but this is the first time I have been shot at.' The fireman, who was in the cab with the driver, said that when they stopped to take on water, he saw three boys nearby, one of whom was carrying an air rifle. On the same day that somebody fired at the train driver, a wooden sleeper was laid across the line near Huyton Station. The driver of a train from Liverpool to Manchester had to stop in order to remove it.

Much of what has been said in this chapter will conflict sharply with the generally-recognized picture of children's play in the 1950s and 1960s. A lot of us see vandalism as a relatively modern scourge and the idea of young train- and planespotters taking part in systematic sabotage of railways lines and airport landing lights is a startling one. Many readers will have a vague idea that the 'feral' child or youth is a relatively recent phenomenon, caused perhaps by soft parents and trendy teachers. One hears it said in all seriousness that the reason that youngsters behave so badly today is that they no longer face the threat of the cane at school or sharp retribution if and when they are hauled before the courts. Such arguments do not really hold water when we look at exactly the same conduct by children at a time when the slipper and cane were being freely wielded by teachers and the courts were all too ready to send those convicted of anti-social behaviour to approved schools or Borstal.

Before turning to another aspect of life for the baby boomers when they were growing up, a word or two must be said about one more serious hazard to children who were 'playing out', one which has now been all but eradicated. The sight of children playing in the streets with fireworks is practically unknown in this country; 'Health and Safety gone mad' has, mercifully, seen to that. Nobody under the age of 18 can buy fireworks, a law which is in the main sedulously adhered to, with shopkeepers requiring age-related identification. Fireworks are fairly expensive too. Apart from boxed selections costing at least £10, there are larger set-pieces, which cost more than the average child would be able to afford. The firework as plaything for children has effectively ceased to exist. This is very different from the way things used to be and readers under the age of 40 will probably be astounded and shocked to learn that fireworks were, well within living memory, very popular toys for children of 10 or 11 and sometimes younger.

The laws which limit and restrict what we can and cannot do seem to change with dizzying swiftness these days and even though most are ultimately for our own good, it can be tricky to keep track of them all. It was not always like this. Until the 1960s, the law relating to the sale and use of fireworks was the 1875 Explosives Act, which had been originally brought in to control the supply of gunpowder being used by Irish terrorists operating in Britain during the reign of Queen Victoria. Nobody had ever thought of changing or amending this law, which seemed quite adequate for the regulation of the fireworks sold in the run-up to Guy Fawkes Night. After all, it had worked perfectly well for almost a century; why alter it? Under the provisions of the 1875 Act, fireworks could only be sold to children over the age of 13. This meant of course that in practice, 11- and 12-year-olds were buying them and then giving them to their younger brothers and sisters.

In real terms, fireworks in the twenty years following the end of the Second World War were incredibly cheap. They were sold individually, many costing only a penny or two: well within the financial reach of most children. If they didn't have the money, then this could usually be raised by begging, under the time-honoured expedient of 'Penny for the Guy'. How cheap were fireworks at that time? Small Roman Candles could be bought for 1d or 2d. This equates to less than 1p in modern currency. Even taking into account the inflation since that time, this would still work out at no more than 15p or 20p. Not only were the fireworks at that time inexpensive, they were also horribly dangerous, both to the children and to those around them. Take the 'banger' for instance, a little tube filled with gunpowder which exploded with a loud bang when lit. These were thrown, dropped into empty milk bottles, fixed to people's cats with rubber bands, emptied out into other containers in order to make a larger explosion and misused in a hundred other ways. They are now illegal in this country. Or what about the jumping cracker; a handy little firecracker which jumped all over the place when lit, emitting bangs as it did so? Small children jumping back in fright from these squibs had been known to leap into bonfires. The jumping crackers also routinely jumped into boxes of fireworks and detonated the whole lot at once. The failure to bring in new legislation to supplement the 1875 law which covered fireworks and children came at a dreadful cost. In an average year today, fifty people are hospitalized through accidents involving fireworks. In the early 1960s, the rate was eight times as high, with most of the victims of firework-related injuries being children.

We have looked in some detail at the practice of 'playing out' and found it wanting. Children were losing eyes, breaking limbs and even being killed, because they were allowed out of the house by their parents at an early age, without any adults accompanying them to see that they remained safe. This was a terrible way to carry on, but social and economic necessity was at the back of it and most families had little choice but to pursue this dangerous and unsatisfactory way of doing things. Today, parents know better and are no longer compelled by circumstance to put their children at hazard in this way.

Having disposed of the notion that 'playing out' was good for the health of children in the 1950s, it is time to consider the health of children at that time generally and see how it compares with the modern world. We are often told that children today are less healthy than those of a few years ago. This strange and counter-intuitive idea will be explored in the next chapter.

Chapter 5

Falling Life Expectancy:
Are the Baby Boomers More Healthy than their Grandchildren?

For at least 500 or 600 years, the life expectancy of people in Britain has risen inexorably. In the Middle Ages, the average life expectancy at birth was perhaps 35 or so. This was due in part to the very high infant mortality rates at that time; many babies did not live to see their first birthday. Childhood was a hazardous business, with around a quarter of children dying before they reached adolescence. By the middle of the eighteenth century, life expectancy had gone up slightly and was about the 40 mark. It was in the twentieth and twenty-first centuries that life expectancy really soared. By the 1930s, men could expect to live until the age of 60 and twenty years later, this had risen to 65. In 2015, the most recent year for which figures are available at the time of writing, men in this country are expected at birth to live to 79 and women to 83. At the beginning of the twentieth century, only 20 per cent of babies born would live past their sixtieth birthday; today, the figure is 80 per cent.

In short, until ten or fifteen years ago, the news for life expectancy in Britain has been increasingly optimistic with each passing year, each successive generation living longer than those preceding it. There seemed no reason to suppose that this happy state of affairs would not continue with the children of the so-called millennials, those born between the early 1980s and the year 2000, living longer than either the baby boomers or their children. The picture was rosy.

According to many newspaper reports, based upon statistics from the NHS and other authoritative sources, this trend towards ever higher British life expectancy is about to be thrown into reverse. Not only will the life expectancy of those born in this country begin to fall, this effect will be dramatic enough to mean that children today are likely to die before their own parents. That such an implausible scenario should be uncritically accepted by many people illustrates once more the powerful grip that the myth of the baby boomers' childhood has upon so many people, including those in the government and National Health Service. In Chapter 3, we saw how laws had been passed which were founded upon a false vision of childhood in the 1950s and 1960s, the 1998 Crime and Disorder Act, which introduced the new mechanism of ASBOs, being a direct response to the perceived menace of children and young people who were believed to be running out of control in an unprecedented fashion. Taking as their model the supposedly less savage children who were around during the 1950s, the new Labour government attempted to tackle what they saw as dangerous and disturbing trends in children's conduct, which could be checked by new laws. Always in mind was the notion of the carefree, happy and inoffensive lives that government ministers had themselves enjoyed. The whole aim was to bring back the pattern of baby boomer childhood, a time when anti-social behaviour and hooliganism were negligible problems. Of course, as we also saw in that same chapter, this vision of childhood in the years after the end of the Second World War is an almost wholly false one. Precisely the same process, that of using a distorted and unrealistic version of the past as a yardstick and deciding that the present is failing in comparison to it, is currently taking place in medical circles, aided and abetted by the government.

Once again, the goal is somehow to recreate the baby boomers' childhood experiences and thus stave off the terrible threats faced by modern children; this time on the health front. The chief fear is of what is sometimes called the 'Obesity Time Bomb', and so relentlessly has the idea been peddled in recent years that there will probably be few readers who doubt that children today are far less healthy than they were fifty or sixty years ago. Indeed, this is taken as almost axiomatic, the starting point for any debate about the welfare and health of children in twenty-first-century Britain. If only the lifestyle enjoyed by the baby boomers could be magically imposed upon the nation's boys and girls, then their health would undergo a miraculous and beneficial transformation.

We shall return shortly to the question of obesity and its deleterious effects upon British children, but first we must consider the strange proposition that children were in any way healthier in the 1950s than they are today. The history of childhood in the baby boomer years is written by those who survived it and flourished. It is time to look at those who either failed to make it to adulthood at that time or whose lives were so wretched that they have no desire to write perkily about the pleasures of staying out until teatime, sometimes because they were physically incapable of achieving any such feat.

In a book entitled *A Mobile Century? Changes in Everyday Mobility in Britain in the Twentieth Century*, the authors interviewed, among others, baby boomers. There are reminiscences about how much fun these people had as children, before 'Health and Safety went mad' and spoiled the enjoyment of simple childhood pleasures like swimming in dirty canals. One woman actually cites swimming in dirty canals, playing in old air-raid shelters and not telling her parents about men who indecently exposed themselves to her as being positive aspects of her childhood. We saw earlier what happened to one little girl who played in an old air-raid shelter; she became an early victim of the paedophile serial killer Robert Black. In the same chapter, we looked also at the advantages or otherwise to children of concealing sexual abuse by adult males. Time now to consider the idea that that swimming in 'dirty canals' might have been a harmless way to while away the hours for children in the post-war years.

One of the recurring features of baby boomer childhood which appears to have been quite forgotten is the terrible epidemics of infectious diseases which swept across the country before the widespread use of vaccines and antibiotics. Today, we regard outbreaks of poliomyelitis, smallpox, TB and diphtheria as tragedies in far-off lands which only affect us when the occasional holidaymaker returns from India or Africa and later manifests some unusual symptoms. They are not something about which we need to worry in the general way of things. It was not always so. Here are one or two statistics which might give readers food for thought. All are taken from the period when the baby boomers were born; that is to say between 1946 and 1964;

- In 1947 there were 8,000 cases of polio in England and Wales.

- Tuberculosis was a big killer throughout the 1950s. In 1950 alone, over 11,000 people died from this disease.

- Three-quarters of a million cases of measles struck Britain in 1961, the vast majority among children.

- Even smallpox outbreaks were not unknown. In Bradford in 1962, six people died after contracting smallpox.

Many of the most contagious diseases which were rife in Britain during the years at which we are looking affected a disproportionate number of children. Some of them, polio and measles for example, were accepted childhood illnesses at that time. Not for nothing was poliomyelitis known also as 'infantile paralysis'. The number of children actually dying from polio and other infectious diseases was relatively low: during the measles epidemic of 1961, although 750,000 cases were recorded, only 150 children died in the outbreak. However, this does not tell the full story. Apart from those who died, many more were left with brain damage or rendered deaf. Despite so many children being left disabled or even dying from catching it, measles was one of the milder illnesses to afflict the baby boomer children. Infinitely worse in many ways was polio.

The death rate from polio, which chiefly affected children and young people, was running in the 1950s at a little under 10 per cent. So we find that in 1953 there were 320 deaths in England, resulting from a total of 4,547 cases of the disease. This is itself shocking. There are no common diseases in Britain today with anything like a 10 per cent mortality rate. For the survivors though, the thousands of children who were not killed by the disease, life could be unbelievably grim. These are adult men and women today whom we seldom hear from when magazines and newspapers run pieces lamenting the fact that childhood for today's children is not a patch on what it was sixty years ago. Not only would these thousands of children not be staying out until teatime, they would not be going out at all for months or years at a time. In some cases, they never went out again after they fell ill, even though they might have lived on for decades.

One of the reasons that parents today do not think it a particularly good idea for their children to go swimming in dirty canals is not that they have become obsessively concerned with Health and Safety, worrying neurotically about trifling dangers that yesterday's children took in their stride. It is rather because we know that many germs thrive in dirty water and that children swimming in such water might swallow these germs or become infected with them through cuts and grazes. It's common sense really. These days, anxieties about dirty canals might focus more upon things such as Weil's Disease or leptospirosis, a bacterial infection spread via rat's urine. For the baby boomers, the greatest fear of parents was polio, which was also transmitted most readily by contaminated water. This is one of the chief reasons why swimming pools began to use chlorine as a disinfecting agent: it reliably destroys the polio virus.

Throughout the 1950s tens of thousands of children in Britain caught polio. More than 90 per cent of them survived, but many suffered varying degrees of paralysis. This could cause limps and wasted muscles; the sight of children with their legs in metal callipers at that time was not an uncommon one. Far worse though was when the muscles most affected were those in the chest which allow us to breathe. In such a case, a child could literally suffocate, a terrible death. Developments in the 1930s had saved countless lives when the respiratory system was paralysed in this way, but this saving of lives came with its own cost.

In the 1920s and 1930s, artificial respirators were developed which mimicked the effect of the chest muscles. These became known as iron lungs. One may be seen in Illustration 14. The pressure within the iron lung was alternately lowered and raised, which caused the lungs to expand and then shrink again. In this way, a victim of polio whose muscles were paralysed could be kept breathing indefinitely. The obvious disadvantage was that the patient had to be altogether enclosed in what amounted to a metal coffin, with only the head projecting from the apparatus.

During the polio epidemics of the 1940s and 1950s, entire hospital wards were crammed with iron lungs, each containing a helpless child. There were over a thousand iron lungs in use in this country. Illustration 15 shows a hospital ward of polio victims in iron lungs in the United States at that time, identical to those in Britain. For some, only a week or two would be needed in the contraption. For others, months or years were needed before their own muscles could take over the function of the electric bellows which ceaselessly pumped air in and out of the machine. Until that time, they were compelled to lay helplessly on their backs, quite unable even to feed themselves, let alone play out all day long. There were those, though, who never recovered the use of their chest muscles. For them, the iron lung was a life sentence and even now there are a handful of people still dependent upon such antiquated machinery. In 1948, 11-year-old Martha Mason fell ill with polio and was confined to an iron lung.

She remained in it until her death sixty-one years later. There are still elderly people in iron lungs to this day.

Here then is one strand of childhood from the time of the baby boomers which those who grew up at that time have chosen to erase from their memories. When expressing enthusiasm about playing out all day, nobody ever troubles to mention the children with leg callipers who were unable to keep up with their playmates, let alone those trapped in iron lungs. Such things are of course unknown today, one way in which the health of British children in the twenty-first century is incomparably better than it was sixty years ago.

The reason that life expectancy has risen so sharply in the last four or five decades is because children, by and large, no longer die before they reach adulthood. This effect is glaringly obvious to anybody who cares to examine the relevant statistics and then compare them with modern figures. Consider for a moment the year in which the post-war baby boom actually began. Today, the death of a baby before his or her first birthday is a rare tragedy. The infant mortality rate in Britain stands at fewer than four deaths per 1,000 for children under the age of one. In 1946, the year that the baby boom begun, ten times as many babies were dying, the infant mortality rate being 45 per 1,000 that year. We reflect again on what was said earlier, about history being written by survivors. One in twenty of those first British baby boomers failed to live even twelve months after their birth.

Infectious diseases were not the only cause of disability and death among children born during the baby boomer era. We looked in an earlier chapter at some of the many grave hazards involved in the practice of playing out, sometimes suggested as a sovereign remedy for the so-called 'obesity epidemic' with which our children and grandchildren are constantly threatened. Other factors to be taken into account when deciding whether children in those days were genuinely healthier than todays' youth are diet and air quality, which, oddly, were associated in causing one particular health problem for the baby boomers.

Until the late 1940s and early 1950s, the deficiency disease of rickets was endemic in this country, particularly in the larger cities. It was said that 80 per cent of British children suffered rickets to a greater or lesser extent at that time. The consequences of rickets could be lifelong and also life-limiting. For those unfamiliar with this scourge, rickets was caused by a lack of calcium and Vitamin D in the diet; it was also greatly exacerbated by a shortage of sunshine on the skin. In order to become rigid and hard, the bones of our bodies need two ingredients. One is calcium in the diet and the other Vitamin D. Without this essential vitamin, the calcium in the diet cannot be utilized for the building of healthy bones.

Many baby boomers suffered from rickets as they grew up. This can cause all manner of difficulties in later life. Sometimes, the external manifestations of childhood rickets are trifling and pose no problems in adulthood. The weight of the child's body on the supporting bones of the legs can make them bend outwards, for example, causing bow legs. Then again, soft bones can result in twisted spines, a condition known as scoliosis. Sometimes the ribs are forced out of shape and the child develops a pigeon chest or hunchback. Deformities such as these, especially combined with scoliosis, can mean that the heart and lungs do not have enough room to operate effectively in the thoracic cavity. This can shorten the life of a sufferer. Those who were children in 1950s Britain might recall that their mothers were given bottles of cod liver oil by health clinics. This is a rich source of Vitamin D.

The body can synthesize Vitamin D when ultraviolet light falls on the skin in sufficient quantities. This happens of course when we go out of doors and expose our skin to the sun. Considering how much time that the baby boomers spent out of doors as children, one would think that they were surely receiving enough sunlight to provide them with all the Vitamin D they needed, without resorting to the expedient of cod liver oil. That they were not and that rickets was commonest of all in cities, brings us neatly to another point about the supposedly robust health which children in those days enjoyed.

The main reason that children in Britain's cities didn't get enough sunlight to stave of Vitamin D deficiency and the rickets which it caused, was that there wasn't nearly as much sunshine in British cities and towns as there is now. In 1950s London, there was an average of thirty-eight hours of sunshine in November. Today, there are seventy hours of sunshine in that month, almost twice as much as there was sixty years ago. The reason for this has not, as might at first be guessed, anything to do with global warming. It is simply that the sunlight was often unable to penetrate the clouds of smoke which hung perpetually over cities at that time.

Children growing up in the 1950s were always enveloped in smoke of one sort or another, whether they were indoors or out. This had, as might well be imagined, a terrible effect upon their health. In fact the smoke even had a bad effect upon children who had not even yet been born. Recent research on the Great Smog of 1952, in which atmospheric conditions combined to trap coal smoke over the capital for four days revealed something surprising.

In December 1952, cold weather in London and a lack of wind meant that smoke from the many thousands of coal fires used to heat people's homes at that time collected over the city and turned into what was known as a 'smog'. The severe air pollution caused many deaths from respiratory disorders. Government statisticians at the time calculated that 4,000 people had died prematurely that winter, although modern research suggests that this was a serious underestimation of the true death toll. A figure of 12,000 has been mooted as being closer to the mark. The very young and very old were the chief casualties of this environmental disaster. One ill effect which has only recently come to light is the effect of this pollution on babies still in the womb.

In March 2016 a paper was presented to the annual conference of the Royal Economic Society. Drawing upon studies of those born after the 1952 smog, it strongly suggested that adults whose mothers were pregnant with them at the time and living in London were 5 per cent less likely to have a degree. Men were 4 per cent less likely to have a job at the age of 50. These may sound like minor effects, but they are nonetheless significant for all that. It seems almost certain that the frequent air pollution from coal fires, which were the almost universal means of heating homes at that time, harmed children who had not even been born and not just during extreme cases of smog. These harmful effects might be elusive, but the difference that smoke made to the health of children at that time was very noticeable. It must be borne in mind that in 1950, 98 per cent of British homes were reliant upon open coal fires to heat their homes. As those millions of fires reduced the coal to ashes, by-products in the form of smoke and soot were simply discharged from chimneys and sent straight into the homes and the atmosphere outside. In addition to this, there were a number of coal-fired power stations operating in London at Battersea, Bankside and Fulham. During the Great Smog, 2,000 tons of carbon dioxide, 370 tons of sulphur dioxide and 140 tons of hydrochloric acid were being pumped into the air over London every day. Because of the meteorological conditions, these injurious substances simply remained suspended in the atmosphere to be breathed in by the city's inhabitants.

The Great Smog was an extreme example of what happened regularly in every city and town in Britain at that time. The air that urban children breathed in was laced with a deadly cocktail of chemicals which did their lungs no good at all. Whether indoors or out, the air was full of sulphur and soot. Added to this was the all but universal habit of smoking. In 1948, 82 per cent of men in this country were smokers and almost every home was filled not only with the smoke from open fires, but also by clouds of tobacco smoke. Not just homes, but shops, cinemas, trains and even doctors' waiting rooms were smoky. It will hardly surprise anybody to learn that respiratory problems for baby boomer children were a serious concern.

It is sometimes claimed that childhood asthma and allergies are on the rise and that this trend is something new and alarming. Yet another disorder of modern life that baby boomer children did not have to contend with! It will perhaps not surprise readers unduly by this time to discover that there is more to this than meets the eye. In the 1950s, as we have seen, the urban air was loaded with substances such as a sulphuric acid, which had no business finding their way into the lungs of children. Every day throughout the winter, 1,000 tons of soot was also entering the atmosphere in London alone, which was duly breathed in by those living in the capital. This is to say nothing of the many tons of hydrochloric acid, suspended in a fine aerosol, which also entered everybody's lungs, along with the ever-present and copious amounts of tobacco smoke. Little wonder then that the irritation of the lungs known as bronchitis was very common in children.

So common was bronchitis that unless it was particularly severe, no parent would have thought to visit the doctor for such a minor ailment. It was just one of those things that one took for granted. It was known throughout the world, after all, as the 'English disease'. The symptoms of bronchitis are almost identical with those of asthma; both are characterized by wheezing and shortness of breath. It seems likely that among the many cases of acute bronchitis seen in children during the 1950s and 1960s, a lot of asthmatics were hiding, their symptoms mimicking almost precisely those of the bronchitis sufferers. The point to bear in mind about bronchitis is that it can, if persistent, cause permanent damage to the lungs. Children growing up in the smoky atmosphere of mid-twentieth century Britain were having their lungs wrecked and their lives shortened, even if it would be decades before anybody was even aware of the fact.

The picture of the health of the baby boomer children so far has not been encouraging. They certainly do not look to have been in better shape than modern children and in many cases, their health was demonstrably worse. What about all the exercise though? Surely this was good for them and prevented them becoming lazy and fat, which is likely to lead to Type 2 diabetes in later life? It is undeniably true, is it not, that in that respect at least, the children of half a century or more ago were doing a good deal better than those born since the millennium?

We come now to one of the greatest of modern myths about childhood; that compared with children of a generation or two ago, today's children are so overweight and get so little exercise that their long-term health is at serious risk. So fixed has this idea become, that it is now accepted as being almost an article of faith, not only among the general public but also with politicians and health professionals. There is an increasing sense of urgency and the feeling that something must be done to save the lives of children at risk of dying prematurely due to their idle and pampered lifestyle.

The feeling that there a crisis in the weight of the nation's children began to become noticeable in the first few years following the turn of the millennium. Articles appeared in newspapers warning that children were heading for disaster in later life. By 2004, MPs were becoming very worried about the fate of British children in the future. In May 2004, the House of Commons Health Select Committee published a report on obesity, which repeated a warning which had already been floating about for two or three years. They claimed that, 'The sight of amputees will become much more familiar. There will be many more blind people.' As this were not alarming enough, the report went on to say that, 'Indeed, this will be the first generation where children die before their parents as a consequence of childhood obesity.' It was all very scary and the thought of all those obese adults stumbling round the streets in a few years' time with wooden legs or carrying white sticks, was enough to provoke several successive administrations to action.

In the 2016 budget, controversy was provoked by the Chancellor of the Exchequer's insistence on the imposition of a 'sugar tax', designed to reduce the consumption of sugar by children. This was allegedly motivated by a strong desire to save the lives of children by preventing them from succumbing to the terrible scourge of obesity and thus having their lives unnecessarily shortened by heart disease and diabetes. Once again, the imagined pattern of baby boomer childhood was being used to dictate policy in the twenty-first century, in this case a perceived need to make modern children as wiry and fit as the baby boomers had been in their youth.

One of the strange things about the obesity 'crisis' among children is that unless we were continually being reminded of it by newspapers and television, most people would not even be aware that such a thing was supposed to exist. Looking at the average class of primary-school children, it does not immediately strike one that they are, on the whole, overweight, let alone morbidly obese. Of course, there are one or two fat children in most classes, but surely that was always the case? The fictional Billy Bunter was based on the fact that there were fat British children about, even a century ago. Despite what is drummed into us relentlessly by the mass media, there is no sign in real life that that there are more fat children than there were a few years ago.

In the Introduction, it was remarked that baby boomer childhood has been officially adopted as the yardstick by which we measure anything at all relating to children in twenty-first century Britain. If we find that fewer children are walking to school than was the case in 1959, that is a problem. If children spend less time reading books than they did in 1955, something must be wrong with modern childhood. When we learn that today's children weigh more or are taller than those sixty years ago, alarm bells should start ringing. It is this instinctive and negative reaction to any aspect of childhood which deviates from the perceived norm, meaning the way things were when senior politicians, judges and doctors were themselves children, which has triggered the 'obesity crisis'. To understand the fuss being made today about children's weight, we must look back once more to the past.

The first thing to realize is that claims that there are more overweight children in Britain than there used to be, are nothing new. This idea was certainly about when the baby boomers were growing up. In October 1960, the radio programme *Any Questions* was broadcast from St Mary's Hall, Arundel. Then, as now, the questions from the audience reflected current anxieties. One of the questions that evening was about how to tackle the growing problem of childhood obesity or, as it was put in those days, what to do about overweight children. This was a very topical subject. Since the end of rationing in the 1950s, sweets came off the ration in 1953, it had been noticed that there were an increasing number of children who appeared to be overweight. Many people believed that the strict rationing during and after the Second World War had been healthy for children and that the large amounts of sugar, in the form of sweets, was now being consumed was creating what we today call an 'Obesity Time Bomb'.

In 1964, the increase in the number of fat children was causing concern for British doctors. On 13 November that year, Dr Otto Wolff, a specialist in child health, told a seminar in Birmingham that overweight children tended to grow into overweight adults and that there was a link between obesity and social class, an idea that is regularly appearing in the media today. Dr Wolff, who was Reader in Paediatrics and Child Health at Birmingham University, said that obesity was the most common nutritional disturbance in the developed world. Interestingly, he raised precisely the same fears about the risk to long-term health among overweight children that we are hearing now, telling the seminar that about four-fifths of obese children would go on to become obese adults and that this had serious implications for an increased mortality rate. The doctor went on to talk of the need for children to engage in more physical activity.

The themes touched upon at the seminar in Birmingham over half a century ago are all very familiar to us; the need for children to get more exercise and the danger of their life expectancy being shortened unless something was done about the problem. Curious indeed to see that such things were already being said when the baby boomers were children.

Worries about weight were still going strong a few years later. If anything, they had intensified. A survey in 1967 found that when asked if they felt that they had weighed more in the last three months than they would like to, 62 per cent of adults replied that they had. In other words, almost two-thirds of those questioned were worried about their weight. Of those who weighed more than they liked, a third said that they first considered themselves overweight as children. In that same year, a clinic for overweight schoolchildren opened in the northern town of Salford. The aim was to help children lose weight by dieting and regular exercise. The medical officer for health of Salford, Dr J. Burn, said that, 'The problem of overweight in the 11–15 age group is increasing'.

We can see by all of this that concerns about overweight children are hardly a new phenomenon. For at least the last sixty years, ordinary people have been fretting about losing weight and worrying that their children weigh too much. Even at the height of the baby boomer era, it was being claimed that children were growing increasingly and unhealthily fat.

What then is the truth of the matter? Can we use the baby boomers' childhood years as a benchmark and try to recreate the lifestyle then in order to reduce the seemingly unstoppable march of childhood obesity? Might it be worth trying to get children to walk to school, turn off the television and play outside more, as a means of saving them from Type 2 diabetes and the blindness and amputation of their limbs which that illness can cause? We saw earlier that life expectancy in Britain has been going up steadily for many years. So too has the height and weight of both children and adults. This is scarcely surprising. The main dietary problem in this country historically has not been being overweight, but malnutrition. During the first half of the twentieth century, the need was to build children up by providing them with nutritious and enriched food, so that they would not suffer from deficiency diseases such as rickets and scurvy. Children tended to be skinny and undersized and this led to all sorts of health problems. With the burgeoning prosperity of the 1950s and 1960s, they began to put on weight, which really should have been a cause for rejoicing, rather than anxiety! As the baby boomers grew up, it became, for the first time in British history, rare to see a seriously underweight and malnourished child. The increasing weight of the baby boomer children went hand in hand with better health and rising life expectancy. That the average child now weighed more than in the 1920s was recognized to be a good thing: they would as a result live longer than their parents and grandparents.

Although it is not strictly relevant to the examination of baby boomer childhood which we are undertaking, it is interesting to see how the present-day 'obesity crisis' among children has been created. It is customary when discussing obesity to mention that in some year in the past people weighed less than they do today. So we are told that the average man in the late 1950s weighed 10.2 stone, as opposed to today's average of 13.2 stone; the inescapable conclusion being that we are a nation of porkers! Of course, if we go back another fifty years or so, we find that the average weight of recruits to the British army in 1900 was less than 9 stone. Perhaps this, rather than the 1950s average weight should be used as our standard when thinking about obesity? What is it which leads us believe that 10.2 stone and not 8.7 stone should be the ideal weight upon which we should found all our hopes and expectations for the future of the nation's children? Why should anything over this be regarded as dangerous?

There are two reasons why Britain has fallen prey to a childhood 'obesity epidemic' and neither have anything particularly to do with the health of the country's children. The first reason that we are reading a lot in newspapers about overweight children is of course that following the trend for the last century or so, children in Britain now weigh more than once they did. This has been a constant process since 1900 or so. Because modern children do not seem to spend as much time out of doors as they did, older politicians, doctors and others have convinced themselves that the increase in weight of their own children and grandchildren must somehow be tied in with an unhealthy lifestyle and that something must be done to get these children to start climbing trees and playing in parks again.

The clinical evidence that children are now unhealthily fat and likely to die at an earlier age than their older relatives is sparse and unconvincing. The main cause of childhood obesity has nothing to do with diet and lifestyle and everything to do with a decision taken in the United States two years before the dawn of the new millennium. One of the easiest and most misleading ways of measuring obesity in a population is by working out the Body Mass Index (BMI) of individuals and then arbitrarily deciding whether this exceeds a certain number and the person is therefore overweight. The BMI is found by dividing the weight in kilograms by the square of the height in metres. This figure is then divided by the height again to yield a number which is typically between 20 and 35. The higher the number, the more likely the person is to be overweight or obese.

This method, which is a notoriously crude way of measuring anything and does not alone yield anything much in the way of objective clinical data, shows once again the difficulty in comparing the situation with childhood now and the way that it was in the 1950s or 1960s. To begin with, nobody in Britain at that time was using the metric system, let alone using kilograms and metres to work out BMIs. Even the term Body Mass Index was unknown before 1972. This means at once that we have no real idea how many fat children were around in this country in 1957, say. We know that there were some, because people were expressing concern about this, but we have no idea if there were more, less or about the same number of overweight children as there are today.

There is another great problem with using BMI as the basis for claiming that there is an obesity crisis and that is that the definition of obesity is not a fixed one, but changes dramatically from one decade to the next. In 1997, for instance, one was officially overweight if the BMI was 27 or over. Then, acting on dubious evidence, America's National Institute for Health decided to lower the threshold from 27 to 25. On Wednesday, 17 June 1998, the new guidelines were introduced and overnight, 25 million Americans became overweight or obese. In Britain too, millions of adults were officially reclassified as being too fat for their own good.

To show the absurdity of this new method of defining obesity, it is only necessary to look at professional athletes such as the American basketball star Michael Jordan. When Jordan was at the peak of his career and a supremely fit player, his waist was just 30 inches. Nevertheless, his BMI ranged between 27 and 29, making him, technically at least, overweight and verging on obese. BMI makes no allowance for muscle to fat ratio or ethnicity. This has led to the parents of slim, healthy schoolchildren being sent letters which warn that their child is in danger of becoming overweight.

On 29 April 2016 Mrs Claire Margeson of Hull, in East Yorkshire, received a disturbing letter from Humber NHS Foundation Trust. As part of the sinister-sounding National Child Measurement Programme, her 10-year-old son Bradley's height and weight had been measured and recorded. The conclusion was stark: the little boy was overweight. The odd thing about all this was that Bradley Margeson certainly did not look in the least overweight in photographs and nor did his weight seem out of the ordinary. The 4ft 8in (143.2cm) high boy weighed just 6st 8lb (41.6kg). Who in their senses could possibly think that this indicated a fat or even chubby child? Fortunately, both mother and child laughed at the absurdity of the thing and so no harm was done. Here is a child who would fit into any photograph of healthy boyhood in the 1950s and yet he has been officially classified as being overweight, presumably one of those poor wretches who will be going blind or having his arms or legs sawn off in later life.

The explanation for this and similar claims that children are overweight or even obese is simple. A child is defined as being overweight if he weighs more than most other children of the same age and sex. This is so obviously a strange way to go about the business, as a brief thought experiment will show. Let us suppose that we are able to travel back in time with all our charts and calculators to the medieval period and measure a large number of children's height and weight. Having calculated the average BMI for the group, we would then, using the current methodology, be obliged to define any child in the 91st centile, that is to say a child whose BMI was greater than 90 per cent of the other children, as being clinically overweight. Never mind that this child, if taken from a hungry or emaciated population might look as skinny as a rake by modern standards; by using modern methods, he would be overweight. What we have is a system which will automatically define a proportion of the children in any population, even those starving to death during a famine, as being clinically overweight or obese.

A comparison of old school photographs of classes of children from the 1950s are very similar to more modern pictures. Both show groups of average-looking children, one or two of whom look a little larger than their classmates. There is really no reason at all to think that more British children are morbidly obese or even just a little tubby than was the case a few years ago. In fact, there is strong evidence to suggest the opposite.

In 2004, the year that the report of the Health Select Committee was published, the one which warned of a generation of overweight children likely to die before their parents, another publication also appeared. This was a government report called the *Health Survey for England 2003*. It shed light upon the obesity epidemic which was about to engulf the country's children by revealing that in 1995 the average weight of English boys under the age of 16 was 32kg (5 stone 1lb). In 2003, it had dropped slightly to 31.9kg (5 stone). The average weight of girls under 16 had indeed risen though; from 32kg to 32.4kg. There may well have been some overweight children in England, there always have been, but the average weight of children had remained almost unchanged, despite the feverish media attention about an epidemic of morbidly obese children.

Another point to bear in mind is that all the available evidence suggests that being a little overweight by today's standards; that is to say having a BMI between 25 and 30, is actually associated with lower mortality rates than for people who are of 'normal' weight! In other words, even if the nation's children were *all* found to be officially overweight, then their life expectancy would actually go *up* rather than *down*!

Once again, when examined calmly and rationally, another of the ways that modern childhood is apparently failing in comparison with the childhood of the baby boomers is shown to amount to nothing at all. The idea that the present generation of schoolchildren will all be stumbling around in a few years, blinded by obesity, parts of their bodies having been surgically removed, before dropping dead in front of their parents, is absurd.

The health of British children is far better than that of their grandparents in any measureable way. They are less likely to die in childhood, will live on average longer than their parents and are less likely to suffer from any number of disorders; from tooth decay and rickets to measles and cancer. No doubt the health of their own children will be better still. Having disposed of another of the popular myths associated with the baby boomers, we turn now to perhaps the most popular misconception of all: that children in the twenty years or so following the end of the Second World War were better educated than children who are at school today.

Chapter 6

Back to Basics:
Has Education Been Dumbed Down Since the 1960s?

The one thing upon which everybody seems to agree when talking about the baby boomers is that they received a much better education than that which their grandchildren are likely to get at modern schools. Grade inflation at both GCSE and A level, together with the general dumbing down of education which has taken place over the last fifty years or so are both standbys of lazy journalists, appearing regularly each year as the latest examination results are published. At other times of the year, newspaper headlines trumpet forth the astounding information that one British adult in five is functionally illiterate. Invariably, articles on this subject are illustrated with old examination questions from the 1950s or 1960, compared with the sort of thing found in this year's GCSEs. Not only are young British adults illiterate, they are also innumerate, probably because of all these calculators, computers and mobile telephones! This is an easy game to play and a little later we will see how it is done, but for now let us look at a question from an 11 Plus paper from the 1950s:

3,755 is multiplied by 25 and the result is divided by 125. Write down the answer.

Only think, this question was set for 10- and 11-year-olds! Most adults today would have to stop and think pretty hard about such a poser and in the 11 Plus, there were whole pages of this kind of thing. Surely this tells us something about educational standards as they were sixty years ago? For contrast, here are a couple of questions from 2014's mathematics GCSE paper for 15- and 16-year-olds:

The mountain K3 is eight thousand and fifty one metres in height
Write the number **eight thousand and fifty one** in figures
Work out ¼ of 24kg

Put like that, it appears plainly obvious that 11-year-olds of sixty years ago were doing more complicated sums than today's 16-year-olds, surely? Talk about dumbing down!

This attitude, that educational standards were far higher in the 1950s than they are today, is at the root of many of the changes in government-dictated practice in schools today. It was the reason that that the National Curriculum was introduced in 1988 and also why reading is now mostly taught by the use of phonics, rather than the whole-word, 'look and say' method which was once very widely used in British schools. More recently, we have seen the return of memorizing multiplication tables by heart being officially endorsed as part of the government's 'war on innumeracy and illiteracy'. All these policy initiatives are predicated on the assumption that the old ways of teaching are best and that we are about to be engulfed in a rising tide of illiteracy or surrounded by adults who are unable to multiply two times two without whipping out their mobiles.

Before examining the myth of the high standards of education achieved in the post-war years, another part of the legendary world of the baby boomers, it might be instructive to see what was happening to the educational system in Britain while the baby boomers were growing up. There are still those who yearn for the return of the selective system which was put into place the year after the first of the baby boomers were born in 1946 and many people seem to think that bringing back streaming or grammar schools would be a good way of tackling what are routinely said to be the appallingly low educational standards in many schools. As usual, the years that the baby boomers were growing up are treated as some sort of gold standard to which we should aspire.

In 1946, when the first batch of baby boomers made their appearance in Britain, the school leaving age was 14. Somewhere in the region of 90 per cent of British children left school at this age without any qualifications at all. They had little choice in the matter. Almost all children attended elementary schools which only taught children up to the age of 14. If you wished to take the School Certificate, the 1930s and 1940s equivalent of GCSEs, you would have to go to a secondary school, the majority of which were private fee-paying establishments. True, the grammar schools, although private, set aside a quarter of their places for scholarship pupils, but these were almost all taken up by middle-class children. The reason was that their entry exams were so stiff that only children who came from well-educated homes or whose parents could afford private tuition really had much chance of passing them and so securing a place at a grammar school. It was, as almost everybody agreed, a grossly unfair system and one which was heavily weighted against working-class children. Not only was there no chance of getting into further or higher education without the School Certificate, it was required for many jobs in offices. The lack of it meant that an awful lot of young people were condemned immediately to a life of manual work, with little prospect of advancement.

The 1944 Education Act was to change all this by raising the school leaving age and making secondary schools freely available for every child in the country. Those who had the ability to benefit from a grammar school education and perhaps university also would be able to do so, regardless of their family's class or income. The rest would attend either technical schools or secondary moderns, where they would receive a good general education, geared to the practical rather than the academic. It was an inspiring vision of a brave new world of opportunity for the nation's children and it is this glorious dream which has become fixed in our minds, rather than the way that the new system worked out in practice, that is to say with almost no change at all in the dreadfully unfair situation for ordinary children's education which existed before the war.

Obviously, not all children have the intelligence to be able to take advantage of a first-class academic education, or so went the reasoning at the time. It would be necessary to devise a way to sort the sheep from the goats and identify those, regardless of their family background or social class, who would be capable of handling a rigorous education designed to fit them out for university or the professions. To do so, a fair test of intelligence would be needed, so that the bright children could be spotted when young and guided into the fast track to academic success. This project, which became known as the 11 Plus, was doomed from the very beginning. Instead of being the means of opportunity to all children in the country, it became in practice a way of ensuring that the middle classes retained their grip on good schools and universities until the 1970s. Far from identifying bright children with great potential, the 11 Plus was a tool for filtering out the children from working-class homes and ensuring that they were compelled to leave school at the age of 15 with literally no qualifications of any kind. These were the ones who 'failed' the 11 Plus, which was taken in the last year of primary school.

Of course, strictly speaking there should have been no question of anybody 'failing' the 11 Plus. Its stated aim was merely to distinguish those children likely to benefit from an academic education and ensure that they received it. From the beginning, the claim was that there would be 'parity of esteem' between grammar schools and the new secondary moderns. Unfortunately for those in authority, ordinary people are often very quick to spot humbug and cant, however it is dressed up; nobody, least of all the children, had any doubt that this was an examination which one hoped to pass.

To appreciate fully what was going on, we need to bear in mind that the claim was made that it was impossible to coach for this sort of intelligence test and that its results had nothing to do with previous education, being designed purely to identify raw intelligence and intellectual potential. All the available evidence, both the recollections of those who took the 11 Plus and later academic research, suggests otherwise. Perhaps it will help if we look at the sort of questions being asked in the 11 Plus. After this, we will discuss the origins of the examination and why it was thought a good idea to separate children in this way at such a young age. Readers might perhaps wish at this point to try a few typical questions from the 1950s. No calculators allowed!

i.   Simplify 7,236 X 5,287

ii.   An aeroplane flies from Glasgow to London in 1 hour 51 minutes at 220 miles per hour. Find the distance in miles.

iii.   Write down the prime factors of 210

It is immediately apparent that questions like this have little to do with intelligence and everything to do with previous education. In other words, those who were in the top stream of a good primary school would be far more likely to be able to answer them than anybody else. Those who had not received an efficient education or extra help from their parents would be absolutely stumped. The child from an under-performing inner-city school would not even be likely to make it off the starting blocks in a test like this. Whatever it was that was being measured in the 11 Plus, it was certainly not intelligence as such! (For readers who have been racking their brains trying to answer the questions given above, the answers are as follows; i. 38,256,732, ii. 407 miles, iii. 2 X 3 X 5 X 7)

In retrospect, it seems quite mad that anybody could have believed that this sort of thing was an indicator of intellectual ability. The ability to carry out long multiplication or find prime factors will tell us more about what sort of education a child has received in the past, rather than what he or she might be capable of in the future. It was seriously claimed at the time that the 11 Plus was an examination for which it was impossible to coach a child, but this was plainly and manifestly untrue.

What else did the 11 Plus consist of apart from mathematics questions? The General Intelligence/Knowledge component of the exam will give us further clues about what was actually being tested and measured and why a disproportionately large number of working-class children did poorly in the 11 Plus. Here are a few more questions from old 11 Plus papers;

> Write a short account (about four or five lines) on any *four* of the Following;
>
> (i)   Everest
> (ii) Westminster Abbey
> (iii) The Gothic
> (iv) William Shakespeare
> (v)   Queen Salote
> (vi) The Maoris

A glance at these questions really does give the game away. How on earth could an acquaintance with Gothic architecture or information about the indigenous inhabitants of New Zealand be thought of as a measure of intelligence? Clearly, the child of middle-class parents from a family living in London would be far more likely to know about Westminster Abbey than the son or daughter of a working-class South Wales mining family. A middle-class child in London might very well have been taken to the Abbey for a visit; he might even have gone to a play by Shakespeare with his parents. There were, in some papers, questions on such things as the proper role of a parlour maid and the correct usage of 'who' and 'whom'. It is worth remarking that an upper-middle class child would have far more chance of knowing about proper grammar and the place of domestic servants than a child from a working-class family. One more example and then we will look at the theoretical basis for selective education as practiced in the years following the end of the war:

The following incidents occur in well-known books you may have read:

(i)   Tom comes down the wrong chimney

(ii)   Jim discovers the chart of Treasure Island

(iii) Crusoe discovers a footprint in the sand

(iv)   Jo visits Laurie for the first time

(v)   Alice drinks from the little bottle

(vi)   Black Beauty hears the hounds

Describe briefly two of these incidents.

Here, the connection between intelligence, class and education is even starker. What sort of 10- and 11-year-olds are likely to be familiar with the plots of *Robinson Crusoe* and *Little Women*? A working-class child from the slums of Liverpool or a boy or girl with university-educated parents, living in a comfortable, middle-class home in a well-to-do London suburb such as Richmond?

We must remind ourselves that, as in so many other areas of modern childhood from diet to personal lifestyle, education at the time when the baby boomers were children is often held up as being a shining example of what we should now be aiming for. If our children could just learn to shout out the answer at once to eight times twelve or learn to read fluently as quickly as their grandparents did by learning their ABCs, then Britain could once more hold up her head when international educational league tables are published. Perhaps if our schools were more like those that we had in the 1950s, then our children wouldn't be lagging behind those of South Korea and Japan, when it comes to mathematical ability! This, at least, is what ministers in charge of the Department of Education seem to believe. To see what was so terribly wrong with schools and the whole educational system at that time, we must look at the architect of the 11 Plus, in a sense the man who designed the whole post-war British educational system, based as it was on selection at the age of 10 or 11.

The problem with the educational system through which the baby boomer children passed in this country was that it was officially founded upon a form of biological determinism, which is to say, the belief that children inherit most of their intelligence from their parents and that there is only a strictly limited amount that education can do to develop this fixed quantity of brainpower. If your parents are slow witted, then there is very little point in your trying to get to Oxford: you might as well resign yourself to life in a less challenging environment; such as a factory or coal mine.

One man was really at the back of the whole idea that children were possessed of a fixed quantity of innate intelligence which they inherited from their parents and which could be measured. This was Cyril Burt, for almost twenty years an educational psychologist for the old London County Council. Burt was later appointed Chair of Psychology at the University of London. His influence was immense. He acted as consultant to the various committees which developed the 11 Plus and his ideas are clearly discernible in the nature and purpose of the examination.

Cyril Burt believed that around 80 per cent of our intelligence is inherited and that there is therefore a limit on the effect that education can have. He also thought that it was possible to measure this intelligence accurately and scientifically. Both these idea are to be found in the structure and use of the 11 Plus. What those who consulted the eminent psychologist could not have known at the time was that Sir Cyril, as he became in 1946, was in fact a fraud who simply invented the evidence which he claimed to have found for the heritability of intelligence. He cited 'degree theses of the investigators mentioned in the text' to support some of his more controversial ideas about intelligence. Researchers later established that many of these documents simply did not exist. Worse still, in his most crucial work Burt named two research assistants as having carried performed a vital role. These two women, Margaret Howard and J. Conway, were mentioned again and again. Nobody had ever met or even seen these two people and after Burt's death it became increasingly obvious that he had simply invented them. It was upon such shaky foundations that the whole edifice of selective education in post-war Britain was raised.

If the children who passed the 11 Plus were not being selected on the basis of their intelligence, then what on earth were the factors which caused one child to gain a grammar school place by this means and another to end up in a secondary modern? Perhaps we should follow the old question asked when investigating a crime! *Cui Bono*?: who benefits from this thing? It is not necessary to search very hard or far to uncover the answer to this question. The immediate and direct beneficiaries of the new examination were, in many cases, the same children who would already have been going to the grammar schools before they had thrown open their doors and stopped charging fees. In the 1950s, over half the children going to grammar schools were from middle-class homes. In the secondary moderns, only 20 per cent of the pupils were from this background. Whereas before, many middle-class parents had had to pay school fees for children at the local grammar school, they now acquired the places for nothing. There are tales of some fathers literally rubbing their hands together with glee when they realized what a huge saving they would make as the provisions of the 1944 Education Act came into force!

The idea when the 11 Plus started was that the most intelligent 20 per cent of children would be identified and given places at grammar schools, but it became obvious very quickly that this wasn't what was happening. For one thing, although between 20 per cent and 25 per cent overall were going to grammar schools, there were very wide regional differences in the numbers passing. In the rural county of Westmoreland, 40 per cent of children passed the 11 Plus, but seventy miles away in Sunderland only 10 per cent were getting to grammar schools. Could it really be true that there were four times as many clever children in the Lake District as there were in a city in the North East?

Of course, if the 11 Plus really was distinguishing the clever children from the dullards, then none of this should have been happening. Why should children living in nice houses be any brighter than those who were in tenement blocks? Why the dramatic difference in the percentages passing the exam based upon geographical location? It was not until the early 1950s that academic researchers provided the evidence which proved what ordinary people had known almost from the beginning; that the 11 Plus was geared towards the needs of well-educated middle-class children and was heavily weighted against working-class children.

In 1952 Philip Vernon, Professor of Educational Psychology at London

University's Institute of Education, published an article in the *Times Educational Supplement*. He demonstrated clearly that far from being an objective measure of intelligence, scores in the 11 Plus could be greatly increased by systematic coaching. It is probable that few people outside the academic world were surprised to hear this! In the same year, F. M. Martin conducted a survey of 1,446 parents of children taking the 11 Plus that year. He discovered a strong correlation between class and attitudes to secondary education. Only 6.7 per cent of clerical workers had not thought much about their child's secondary education; 33.9 per cent of unskilled workers had not thought about it. 82.7 per cent of professionals had thought a lot about child's secondary education; only 35.3 per cent of unskilled workers had. This concern or lack of it was expressed in coaching and getting child to practice sums and compositions, which made all the difference to the test when it was taken. When added to the culturally-enriched background of such children, which gave them the edge in some of the kind of questions which we saw above, this was enough to give children whose parents had a professional or managerial background a distinct advantage when sitting the 11 Plus.

It has been necessary to go into the background to the British educational system at it was between 1945 and 1965 in order to show that it was deeply flawed, to say the least of it. It could hardly have been otherwise, when the man upon whose work and ideas so much of the schooling in this country was based was a cheat and a fraud. Everything about the system at that time was based upon phoney data and false notions about intelligence. That anybody in the world today, least of all those now in charge of British education, should feel that here was a way of schooling which could be profitably emulated is more than a little staggering!

Before looking more closely at one or two of the strongly-held myths about the way that educational standards in Britain have fallen since the end of the Second World War, we might spare a thought for the thousands of children who did not even get the opportunity to attend the ordinary schools of post-war Britain. These days, we are so used to children who are blind or in wheelchairs, even those with learning difficulties, attending mainstream schools, that we might recall for a moment that this was not at all how things were during the time of the baby boomers. It was routine in the 1950s and 1960s for children who were blind, deaf, suffered from cerebral palsy or had even slight learning difficulties to be sent away from home to boarding schools and long-term institutions. Former Home Secretary David Blunkett is a good example of what could happen to a child who had the misfortune to be born blind.

In 1947 David Blunkett was born into a working-class family in the northern English city of Sheffield. He was born blind. We hear so many jolly tales about the happy life of healthy and able-bodied baby boomers born at this time, that it is sobering to reflect upon the experiences of a blind child in those days. There was no provision in ordinary schools in the 1950s for children who were unable to see and so the only available option for young David was to be sent to a school for the blind. This meant residential accommodation: a boarding school. At the age of just four, the little blind boy was sent away to a boarding school where his parents could only visit him once a month. While he was at school when older, Blunkett was told that the only career open to a working-class blind youth like him was that of lathe operator.

This experience of being sent off to a boarding school and kept there for years was not an uncommon one for disabled baby boomer children. There were schools for 'cripples', for 'the deaf', 'the blind' and also 'the mentally handicapped'. In the case of children with learning difficulties, parents were often persuaded that it would be for the best if their child were to be sent off to an institution for good. Such places were all too often bleak and uncaring, and sometimes cruel. Residential, long-stay hospitals catered for all ages from toddlers to adults. Once they had been put away in institutions like these, which were frequently in remote and difficult-to-get-to rural areas, many parents visited infrequently and sometimes not at all. When large, residential hospitals and homes were being dismantled in the 1980s, as part of the 'care in the community' initiative, adults were found living there who had arrived as three or four-year-olds and were still there thirty or even forty years later. When baby boomers today talk lyrically about the wonderful schools which they attended, the establishments which taught them so much and which were so much more effective than modern schools, we may take it for granted that they are not referring to the schools for the blind or otherwise disabled, to which little boys and girls were shipped off and forgotten.

Let us now see in detail what one of the chief claims that educational standards have been dumbed down since the days when the baby boomers were attending school actually amount to. As popularly understood, the story is roughly as follows. Fifty years ago, the literacy rate in Britain was practically 100 per cent. Almost all children left school able to read and write, as well as being able to calculate the change from a £10 note in their heads. Education was more structured in those days and it was recognized that not all would have prizes. Those children who were able to benefit from it and worked hard were offered a first-class academic education which could lead them on to university and success. Today, probably as a result of trendy, left-wing teaching methods, 20 per cent of children leave school functionally illiterate. They have become so dependent on calculators that many are unable to carry out the simplest arithmetical operation by themselves. As a direct consequence of the pitiful state of the country's maintained schools, almost half the students at Oxford and Cambridge are from private schools. The remedy is to turn back the clock and recreate the style of schooling which was around fifty years ago. This, in a nutshell, is the theory to which many people subscribe and has become official government policy over the last few years. Perhaps if we look at the individual components of this tapestry of myths and half-truths, we shall be able to see what is really going on.

We begin with one of the most frightening of the statistics bandied around about the woeful state of modern British education, that a fifth of the young people in the country are functionally illiterate. This is so often asserted that it has become accepted almost as a fact, but the truth is rather complicated. When we look back at the past and try to work out whether conditions were better or worse at such and such a time, it is of course vital that we are able to measure the things at which we are looking objectively. In the case of literacy, this is impossible to do.

What is usually meant by literacy in Britain today is not the ability simply to read and write, but really the possession of a GCSE in the subject of English Language at Grade C or above. This indicates a reasonable level of literacy, which means that a person can read bus timetables and extract information from a newspaper article in order to answer questions about it. A recent GCSE in English required pupils to plough through an article from the *Guardian* on the subject of prison reform and then answer some pretty deep questions about the views expressed there. One may however be unable to gain a Grade C in an English GCSE or this sort and still be perfectly capable of reading simple texts with complete accuracy, as well as obtaining information from everyday sources. In this way, a person who has not passed a GCSE in English, but still manages to hold down a job in a shop, can be classified as illiterate, at least by modern criteria.

All this is a little confusing and shows how tricky it can be to compare one era with another. Looking back at the baby boomer years, we have no way at all of calculating the literacy rate. Between 1945 and 1965, three-quarters of secondary school pupils in this country did not take, let alone pass, a single examination. This is something which is almost always forgotten when people are extolling the virtues of the British educational system fifty or sixty years ago. Something over 75 per cent of secondary school pupils attended secondary modern schools and left at the age of 15. There were no facilities for such young people to sit O levels, the General Certificate of Education, which was taken at the age of 16. The great majority of adults in the 1950s, 1960s and 1970s had no qualification at all which would allow anybody to make even a tentative guess as to their literacy level.

Another reason that it is not possible to make any meaningful comparison between the proportion of adults who were illiterate in, say, 1959 and now is that different levels were used to judge the matter. In 1959, illiteracy meant just that: a person who could not read or write. The definition of literacy for decades after the end of the Second World War was the ability to read or write a simple note. Judged by this standard, over 99 per cent of adults in Britain fifty years ago were literate, just as they are today.

This is where the faulty recollections of baby boomers have had a huge and abiding influence upon practically every child in the country over the last ten years or so. Once literacy began to be defined in terms of how many teenagers pass an English GCSE at Grade C or above, it becomes clear that a substantial proportion lack the ability to do so. In other words, by this quite arbitrary standard, which has only been around for a few decades, a feeling has arisen that Britain's educational system is failing. A corollary of this is that if children are failing to learn to read and write properly, then this must surely be because they are not being taught correctly. If that is the case, then we must appoint somebody to lead an investigation into the matter and find out what has gone wrong, what is causing this supposed epidemic of illiteracy.

Here is a recent scare story about this subject, indicating that children are starting school less able to learn than they once were and without the necessary skills which will enable them to start acquiring literacy at an early age. A survey carried out in early 2016 by The Key, an information and advice service for head teachers, estimated that almost 200,000 children would be starting school in September 2016 ill-prepared to begin learning. This was shocking news, although examining the data in detail was reassuring. Four out of five teachers were worried about poor social skills and many said that levels of reading, writing and numeracy were lower than 'they should be'. What level of reading, writing and numeracy should children starting school have? Apparently nobody, not even those working for The Key, have any idea. Fergal Roche, who works for The Key said that, 'An agreed definition of what "school readiness" means could be the first step to helping schools, parents and early years practitioners identify what support is needed to meet this growing issue.'

In other words, there is currently no objective measure of how literate or numerate children should be when they start school, but 200,000 of them would fall below this minimum expectation, if it existed! This would actually be quite funny if it were not for the fact that people take nonsense like this seriously and it is the sort of thing that governments are liable to seize upon when next they seek to impose some new diktat upon schools.

Once again, we are told that a problem is developing or getting worse, based upon no evidence at all beyond the vague recollections of middle-aged men and women of how they think their own school days were. As a matter of fact, in the 1950s, children were expected to bring no knowledge at all of literacy to school with them when they began formal education. It was thought to be positively harmful in those days for parents to try and anticipate the job of the school by inculcating in their children the rudiments of reading or arithmetic.

Whenever discussion turns to higher education in this country, the percentage of students who attended state schools and then went on to Oxford and Cambridge Universities is sure to come up. Conclusions are drawn about the quality of British state education by the fact that just over half of Oxbridge students attended ordinary, maintained schools. The rest were educated privately. In other words, the 7 per cent of young people who have been at independent schools are able to take half the places at Oxford and Cambridge. What can possibly be going on in our state schools to produce such a grotesque situation? Perhaps if the state schools were as good as the private ones, then more children from working-class or ethnic minority backgrounds would have the chance of getting to the best universities? And of course, 'improving' state schools always means doing our best to replicate what we suppose the conditions and educational methods to have been in the baby boomer years!

Once again, our collective memory is playing us false. Today, it is admittedly very hard for a pupil from an underperforming state school to get into Oxford. It is *possible* though, as is proved each year when young people from even the most wretched and failing schools somehow overcame all the cultural and educational obstacles in their path and receive offers from Oxbridge. However, fifty-five years ago, it was quite literally impossible for over three-quarters of the children in Britain even to aspire to such a thing. The reason for this was the entrance examinations operating at both universities.

Entry to Oxford University meant having to pass examinations in Latin, Greek and mathematics. This was called Responsions. Cambridge had similar entrance examinations. Obviously, only those at private schools or grammar schools would be studying these dead languages, without which there was no possibility of getting into Oxbridge. For the first fifteen years after the end of the Second World War, this remained the case, effectively barring from those universities over 75 per cent of state school pupils. Even when Latin and Greek were dropped from the entrance examinations, matters did not improve for the great majority of state school pupils, because they were still leaving school at 15, without the opportunity to take even a single examination.

Having dealt with two of the common misconceptions about schooling and education at the time we are examining, we can now look at another strange idea, which is that young people left school at that time with a superhuman talent in mental arithmetic. We hear that all manner of feats were undertaken in this field by ordinary shopkeepers and petrol-pump attendants and that without a calculator, they could multiply two shillings and eight pence by 34 and then tell you what your change should be in farthings. These folk memories can only be based upon garbled anecdotes from old people. Since almost 80 per cent of school-leavers had no qualification of any kind in mathematics, it is very difficult to know how we might be able to say whether they were better, worse or about the same compared to modern youths when it came to arithmetical operations. We have literally no information on this subject.

All of which leads us neatly to the examples which were given above of sums from the old 11 Plus and their apparent superiority to the problems set in modern GCSEs in mathematics. By now, readers have probably worked out how this trick, routinely played on newspaper readers, actually works. It is first necessary to know that between 75 and 80 per cent of children did not pass the 11 Plus. So the questions asked in the examination were not at all of the type that most children would be able to answer, even back in the 1950s. Those who did get them right were those who had been taught well and had a good grasp of arithmetic. There are certainly 11-year-olds today who would make short work of a question which required them to list the prime factors of a large number, but they are, as then, a minority. This is the first stage of the trick; to imply that children in the 1950s or 1960s were all capable of some complicated, arithmetical operations and the fact that many school pupils today can't perform these is an infallible sign that educational standards have fallen over the last fifty years.

The next step is quite neatly done. Having begun by showing a question that very few children would have been able successfully to tackle in the past, we contrast it with one that almost every GCSE pupil in a modern British school will be able to do; for example, writing eight thousand three hundred and fifty in figures. The first one or two questions in the Foundation level GCSE paper are always very simple. The old O level mathematics, which was abolished almost thirty years ago, was something of a blunt instrument. Although it was theoretically divided into grades, nobody really took any notice of them. Essentially, one either passed an O level or failed. If somebody had five O levels, nobody ever troubled to ask about what grade had been achieved; it was enough that one had passed them. The GCSE is a finer tool, which discriminates carefully between various levels of ability. This, combined with the fact that the modern British system allows any child from any background to aspire to a place at university, suggests that any changes in that particular field have been for the better.

It might be amusing to dispose of one very popular belief about modern schoolchildren which baby boomers always seem keen to recycle. This is that children today are so reliant upon computers and calculators that they have no grasp at all of the essential arithmetical operations. In short, they simply punch numbers into a calculator or mobile phone and the answer comes up automatically. They don't really understand what they are doing, which indicates how feeble and deficient their education must have been. In the old days, it is confidently asserted, children could carry out long multiplication on paper, because they had been properly taught and knew what they were doing. This particular piece of nonsense often appears in newspapers when the concept of 'dumbing down' in education is being considered.

In the fantasy world which has been created by the baby boomers, long after the event, any 12-year-old child who wished to multiply 16.82 by 19.61 would set out a proper sum like this;

16.82
19.61 X

The boy or girl would then elaborately work through the digits until the answer was obtained. This is of course absolutely absurd and not at all what would have happened fifty years ago. In fact, the pupil would have reached for a handy aid which would enable this multiplication to be carried out in a far easier way; the 1950s and 1960s version of the electronic calculator. Just like their present-day counterparts, when faced with a tricky sum, the baby boomers would rely upon shortcuts and techniques which hardly any of them understood. A classic case, over half a century ago, of 'dumbing down'!

It is probably a safe bet that no reader under the age of 50 has ever had occasion to use log tables. Indeed, they will probably not even know what they are! Never the less, for many years and certainly for the whole of the baby boomer era, log tables, along with similar tables for Tan, Sin and Cos, were what one turned to when faced by tricky mathematical problems. Not one pupil in a thousand who used the things had any idea how they worked, simply using them as a magic shortcut to tedious number work.

It is beyond the scope of the present book to go into detail about how log tables were constructed. Their use, though, was simplicity itself. Taking the example above, that of multiplying 16.82 by 19.61, one would look up 16.82 in the table and find that a long string of digits was given. The process was repeated for the second number and then the two figures so obtained were added together. The total was then checked in another part of the log table and would show what the answer to the complicated long-multiplication sum would have been. Although children in primary schools were taught long multiplication, just as they are in schools today, by secondary school none would actually be setting out sums in this way. Instead, they used the log tables at the back of their maths textbook.

The important point to bear in mind here is that very few pupils fifty years ago had the faintest idea how log tables were devised or even what they were doing when they used them. It was sheer magic, just like calculators today. They looked up the numbers, added them together and hey presto, no need for any tiresome long multiplication. The same could be said for the use of slide rules, which were also widely used before the development of electronic calculators and computers. Baby boomers used these gadgets as a quick way of doing sums, often not knowing what they were doing.

The present obsession, driven almost exclusively by the distorted recollection of school in the days of the baby boomers, for memorizing times tables by heart, performing mental arithmetic and learning to read by phonics is not motivated by evidence-based research into what constitutes a good and sufficient education. A recent piece of research has revealed how pointless and indeed sometimes counter-productive are the efforts by politicians to compel schools to somehow 'return to basics' and use teaching methods which were around in the post-war years.

For the last twenty years or so, the teaching of reading by phonics has been officially endorsed, as part of efforts to tackle the imaginary scourge of illiteracy which we have been persuaded is threatening the country's economic prosperity and intellectual well-being. It is government policy that it is desirable and wise for children to be taught to read by sounding out the letters of a word, going, 'Cah, Ah, Ter spells "cat"'. It has been claimed that this old-fashioned way of teaching reading has been stunningly successful and that by bringing back the classroom methods which the baby boomers remember so well, we will be able to eradicate illiteracy. This is yet one more example of the way in which the hazy memories of the 1950s and 1960s are used as the basis for policies which will affect millions of people in this country.

The London School of Economics conducted the largest study of the use of phonics in the teaching of reading in British schools, analysing the performance of over a quarter of a million children, whose performance was tracked throughout their primary education. When the results of this massive piece of research were released in April 2016, it was found that although children's scores in reading were boosted immediately after phonics training, this effect disappeared by the time they were tested at the age of 11. By that age, there was no measurable difference in the literacy of those who had been taught with phonics and others who had learned by different methods. The whole drive towards phonics had been a pointless waste of time because, as the researchers noted, 'most children learned to read eventually, regardless of teaching method'.

What we are really seeing all too often in the field of education is a general longing for some non-existent past, a time when all 11-year-olds could calculate in their heads the cost of 36 radiograms at £29 7s 6d each and then go on to work out how much the resulting amount of £1,057 10s 0d would yield in three years if invested in a Friendly Society at 2¾% per annum compound interest. It need hardly be said that although there have always been children and adults capable of amazing feats of mental arithmetic, most of us now, as in the past, have always needed physical aids, whether in the form of a calculator, log table, slide rule or just a simple pencil and paper. The feeling persists, though, among many older people that using digital devices is somehow cheating and leads to an enfeebled intellect and declining mathematical ability. This strange idea is not a new one.

Successive innovations in technology have always been viewed with suspicion by the older generation; especially in as far as they affect children and their studies. Socrates did not like the idea of written works of science or philosophy. When children could read papyrus scrolls, instead of memorizing poetry and history, it was seen as weakening their mental powers and making them intellectually lazy. After all, their parents and grandparents had had to learn by heart entire texts; surely it was cheating to have the things written down, where they could look at them whenever they pleased? The baby boomers, having not had the advantage of access to calculators and the Internet, are now similarly outraged at the thought of children not memorizing a whole lot of things, but rather having them available on tap, so to speak. One quite sees their point. In the early 1950s, children were compelled to learn the names of the royal houses of England, starting with Normandy and going all the way through the Plantagenets and Tudors to Saxe-Coburg-Gotha. Now, any children wishing to know who followed the Normans need only glance at their smartphone and there it is. To an awful lot of baby boomers this smacks of laziness or even cheating!

We shall look next in detail at the mistrust and dislike which older people have regularly evinced for any new medium which their children take a fancy to, from printed books to Internet sites. This is relevant to our main theme and will tell us something about the reason why the childhood of the baby boomers has come to occupy such a place in the perception of the public.

Chapter 7

There Was Nothing Like That
When I Was a Boy!:
The Older Generation's Fear of New Media

It is probably fair to say that very few readers will be familiar with, or even have heard of, The Children and Young Persons (Harmful Publications) Act 1955. This piece of legislation, though, is worth considering both for the light which it sheds on the baby boomer years and also the insight it furnishes into the neuroses of our own age, of which more later.

In a previous chapter, we looked at one or two of the moral panics which have gripped the country over the last sixty years or so; those relating to what was once called 'juvenile delinquency'. We saw that there is nothing new about fears that children and young people today are running wild and that such anxieties are more a psychological disorder of adults, rather than a sociological phenomenon of actually increased violence and criminal behaviour among those under the age of 18. Other types of moral panic about childhood and adolescence are also to be found in our newspapers, although they are not generally recognized as such. It is in the nature of such things that we tend to realize only in retrospect that this or that fear was really groundless. Looking at a couple more of the moral panics from the post-war years might help us to place modern worries in perspective; such things as 'sexting' and the supposedly negative influence of the Internet, social media and electronic devices generally on developing minds.

A recurring theme so far has been the way in which children of earlier generations are seen by adults as having been more active, virtuous and innocent than those of modern times. The 1950s are often seen as a more innocent and healthy time for children and teenagers, who spent their days playing in the park instead of 'sexting', becoming obsessed with violent computer games or accessing inappropriate content on the Internet. There is an underlying fear here, which links worries about obesity with the moral development of children. If they are laying on their beds looking at tablets and mobiles, then they won't be out of doors and engaging in healthy pursuits. It seems clear to us that this is a recipe for idleness, combined with an undesirable obsession with violent or sexual imagery. Their childhood is being stolen from them; they are losing both their innocence and their physical health. It is all so very different from the way in which we ourselves grew up!

Apprehensions that children are becoming lazier and more prone to think about sex than was once the case are nothing new. As far back in British history as we care to go, we find similar concerns about the moral welfare of youngsters and the material to which they are being exposed. Frequently, this goes hand in hand with the fear that not only are their characters being harmed by a preoccupation with unsuitable matters, but that this also causes a physical decline in strength and vitality. Before exploring this topic as it affected the baby boomers, let's have a look at a very modern example of the current hysteria about a new medium which is apparently causing out children to become enervated and weak.

In December 2015, Bob Drew, the head of an infants' school in East London, claimed that children were starting at his school with hands too weak to grip a pencil. Not only were their muscles too feeble to hold a pencil, they also had poor upper body strength as well. The handwriting of children at his school, Gearies in Barkingside, was as a result spidery and uncertain. For Mr Drew, appointed OBE in 2009 for services to education and an adviser to the government on the subject, the cause of the problem was plain. It was digital technology. Specifically, it was small children being allowed unlimited access to ipads and other tablets; what Mr Drew described as 'soft touch' technology. Children spending their time using such gadgets, he suggested, ended up not getting sufficient exercise; with muscles consequently remaining under-developed.

This of course is really nothing at all to do with childhood development and everything to do with fear of a new medium. Books are the ultimate in 'soft touch' technology, requiring only the occasional light brush with one finger to refresh the page. Would this headmaster have been so concerned had his pupils been spending a lot of their time reading? It seems unlikely. Just imagine a school head who was complaining publicly of the harm being done to his pupils' handwriting and general development by the pernicious habit of reading! He would soon be identified as something of a crank. In fact, he is not a crank, just a man following in an ancient tradition of rejecting and denouncing new ways for children and young people to spend their leisure time or acquire information. This custom, and we shall shortly look in detail at its manifestation during the baby boomer years, may be noted as far back as 500 BC. This was when the Greek philosopher Socrates was complaining about a modern medium which he believed was, although he didn't of course use these actual words, rewiring the brains of children. Readers will perhaps be aware that this is currently a fear among many adults that new methods of acquiring information and communicating with each other are having a deleterious and harmful effect upon children's neurological development. Socrates was not worried about mobiles and tablets: his anxiety centred around quite another medium.

In the dialogue entitled *Phaedrus*, recounted by Plato, Socrates and Phaedrus bump into each other on the outskirts of Athens and have a long conversation about various topics. One of these is writing and Socrates criticizes the practice, especially when used educationally, explaining that dead words which are captured on parchment in that way are pretty useless for learning. They are, he asserts, no substitute for human dialogue and live teaching. Elsewhere in ancient writings, we find complaints that the habit of writing things down is harming young minds, by damaging the memory. Instead of remembering huge chunks of poetry or scripture, children can now 'cheat' by having it all written down in front of them. These are the earliest instances of people trying to persuade us that a new medium will harm young minds, although one would be hard-pressed today to find anybody who felt that way about writing!

Returning to this country, we find that in the early sixteenth century; not long after William Caxton introduced printing to this country, there began the proliferation of printed matter, sheets of paper which many older people now argue are far better for young and developing minds than words appearing on electronic screens. One of the results of setting up printing presses in Britain was that for the first time, cheap printed material became available to ordinary people, including children. Some of this related to religious and educational matters, an awful lot was designed to be pure entertainment. Among the most popular productions were chapbooks. These were little leaflets of very poor quality, illustrated with crude woodcuts, which contained ballads, songs, myths and fairy tales. Some were also published about famous crimes and there were smutty sexual adventures as well, the forerunners of pornographic magazines. Inevitably, chapbooks fell into the hands of children and adolescents, who often found them more interesting than the religious texts that they usually encountered, there being no clear division in the early days of printing between works for adults and those intended for children. In 1528 William Tyndale, the religious reformer who translated the Bible into English, complained about the increasingly common practice of allowing young people to read what they pleased: 'Robin Hood and Bevis of Hampton, Hercules, Hector, and Troylus, with a thousand histories and fables of love and wantons and ribaldry, as filthy as heart can think, to corrupt the minds of youth withal.' It is difficult to imagine anybody today who might disapprove in such strong terms of children reading tales from Greek mythology! The new medium, in this case printed books, was clearly thought to pose a moral threat to youngsters, causing them to read 'filthy' stories and so be corrupted.

Fast-forward 300 years to the late eighteenth and early nineteenth centuries and we find serious concern being expressed about the habit of reading novels, which were now becoming widely available. This was believed to be particularly damaging for girls, leading as it did not only to idleness, but giving rise also to an unhealthy interest in romance and sex. Experts warned that girls and young woman became so absorbed in novels that they lost touch with the real world and were eventually unable to distinguish between fact and fiction.

As the nineteenth century drew on, a new menace to the psychological health of young people appeared. These were the so-called 'Penny Dreadfuls', which were similar in many ways to the Tudor chapbooks. These were serialized stories in the form of magazines: the adventures of highwaymen, supernatural thrillers, true crime and various other types of publication. On the covers were lurid, sometimes gruesome illustrations. An enormous industry grew up to provide youngsters with a ready supply of this Victorian pulp fiction and it was blamed for everything from the idleness of errand boys to rapes and murders which had taken place after youths had been reading them. There were demands for 'Penny Dreadfuls' to be prohibited by law, as they were responsible for so much misery.

By the outbreak of the First World War in 1914, the 'Penny Dreadful' scourge had faded away. At its height, youths charged with murders had blamed their crimes on the reading of 'Penny Dreadfuls', an eerie foreshadowing of what became known in the USA in the early years of the twenty-first century as the '*Grand Theft Auto* defence'. This was the claim that the constant playing of the violent computer game *Grand Theft Auto* had blurred the boundaries of some young people's perceptions of reality, to the extent that they had not realized the seriousness of real-life murder. The next menace to the mental stability of the more easily-influenced young person had emerged at the beginning of the twentieth century and was also to be blamed for all manner of ills, from stealing cars to a decline in reading among children. This was the cinema.

In 1913, it was claimed that children's libraries in the city of Nottingham were seeing 50 per cent fewer books being borrowed. The reason, it was alleged, was that children were now spending all their spare time at the cinema and no longer had any time to read library books. Within a few years, the majority of British children were keen cinema-goers. In Edinburgh in the 1930s, 70 per cent of children went at least once a week to the cinema and in London, 63 per cent of under-fives went regularly. Cinemas were blamed for a rise in criminal activity by children, partly because they were emulating the scenes that they saw depicted on the screen. Youngsters brought before the courts for theft claimed that they had stolen money so that they could spend more time at the cinema.

There is a common thread running through fears about chapbooks, novels, 'Penny Dreadfuls', cinema films and tablets, one that has very little to do with any real anxieties that are expressed, but is more about the general uneasiness that adults feel about what children are getting up to amuse themselves. It is a general, rather than particular anxiety. One is irresistibly reminded of a cartoon which appeared in the magazine *Punch* many years ago. A mother is sitting on a beach and saying to a girl aged about 12, 'Go and see what your little brother is doing and tell him to stop it!' It is not so much that William Tyndale in the sixteenth century or Bob Drew in our own have really thought about the harm caused to children by ipads or chapbooks, but that they felt a visceral distrust of and antipathy towards new media that were not available to them when they were themselves children.

All of which brings us to the baby boomer years. Today, we know that the use of relatively new technology such as computers, tablets and mobile telephones is often cited as a contributory factor to everything from obesity and decline in reading standards to violent or prematurely sexualised behaviour in children. We look back to the time within living memory when children spent the whole day out playing and then came home and read the Narnia books or *The Famous Five* with a torch under the bedclothes. How things have changed; and not for the better!

In January 1950 Hephzibah Menuhin, sister of the world-famous violinist Yehudi Menuhin, announced that she was very pessimistic about the future of American children, because as she said: 'Children in America have lost the art of entertaining themselves. They sit by the television set watching horrible, blood-curdling series, and chewing gum. They are lazy, lethargic and completely lacking in initiative.' Alter a few words here and there and this could have been taken from today's newspaper; a description of the ill effects of the Internet, ipads or computer games.

In Britain, people were beginning to say much the same about television, especially as more and more homes acquired television during the 1950s. There were three principal objections to television as a means of entertaining children and young people. In the first place, as Yehudi Menuhin's sister had remarked, this was an essentially passive medium. No imagination was necessary, one did not need to use creative powers to conjure up a picture, as is necessary when reading books or even listening to the radio. With television, the whole thing is done for us. This was said to harm children's natural development and actively work against their ability to think for themselves. To use a modern expression, it was thought that this new medium was in some way 'rewiring' children's brains. Another perceived problem was the time being spent slumped in front of the television screen. This reduced levels of physical activity and some experts said that such a sedentary lifestyle would lay the children open in later life to a raft of disorders including obesity.

Much of this will sound uncannily familiar to modern readers. A nation of couch potatoes who are not using their imagination and cannot be bothered even to read. It is of course precisely what we are now being told every day in our newspapers about the dangers of digital technology. A third aspect of television's effects will also resonate with what is now being said about the Internet and computer games and their effects upon children. Studies in America by the National Association of Educational Broadcasters drew attention to the number of murders and the amount of violence shown on television, in fictional police shows for instance. This coincided with a rise in violent crime and anti-social behaviour by teenagers and older children. A causal link was suspected between the amount of violence seen on television and the propensity of a young person to indulge in aggressive behaviour. We saw this being suggested when the boy accused of the murder of Iris Dawkins was questioned by the police. That he talked of all the murders he had seen on television was thought by some people to be sinister and highly indicative of the malign influence of this new medium on children.

To those people who have bought into the cosy, traditional picture of baby boomer childhood, it might come as a bit of a shock to discover that quite a few adults at the time were already fretting then about what they saw as the deteriorating quality of life for children in the post-war world. Where America leads, Britain invariably follows, at least on cultural matters. It was not long before the supposed link between the spread of television-watching among children and the surge in juvenile delinquency, what we would today call anti-social behaviour by children and youths, was noticed and causing alarm in this country. Older people recalled the days before there were cinemas, radios and television sets and told anybody who would listen how childhood in the 1950s was not what it had been in the 1890s or the Edwardian period.

Television in the 1950s was strongly suspected to be making Britain's children lazy and unimaginative, to say nothing of feeding them a diet of violence and sex and also making them prone to anti-social behaviour. This was bad enough, but as more and more homes acquired television sets, there emerged another fear. Again, it is one which will be familiar to modern readers. Television was said to be harming academic achievement, as well as being responsible for a decline in reading and a loss of interest in activities outside the home. All that children wished to do was slump in front the screen all evening. This was sufficiently worrying that several surveys were undertaken, which examined the views of both children and parents about the increase in television-watching. By 1959, 60 per cent of homes in this country had television sets and within another two years, the figure had reached 80 per cent.

Writing in the *Sunday Times* in 1958, anthropologist Geoffrey Gorer was alarmed that ownership of television sets appeared to be proliferating among the working classes. This was a bad thing, he thought, because unlike middle-class viewers who watched ballet, serious music and documentaries, the working classes seemed to prefer serials and films. Not only that, more than half of them were what Gorer classified as addicts; people who watched for more than four hours a night. This 'gross indulgence' led, at least according to Gorer, to a life 'emptied all nearly all its richness and warmth'. This was because, as a survey that year revealed, in 60 per cent of the homes where there were children and televisions, the set was switched on all evening. As Gorer remarked in his series of articles in the *Sunday Times*, this was not a good thing educationally because, as he put it, it resulted in, 'children's education often imperilled by the absence of any quiet place to do homework.'

So great were worries about children sitting for hours in front of a flickering screen that two major surveys were conducted in the late 1950s on children's viewing habits and the possible ill-effects of excessive screen time. An academic called Heidi Himmelweit produced *Television and the Child*, which did not really come up with any new or surprising insights. For instance, Himmelweit found that although television stimulated interests, these were of the most fleeting nature and tended to lead nowhere. The survey found one or two disturbing facts, such as that in homes with televisions, three-quarters of 10- and 11-year-olds watched until 9.00 pm every evening, which didn't leave them much time for doing anything else. It was also discovered that the violence and bloodshed of the American television series and films which were watched had a dulling effect upon the children's sensibilities and that they hardly cared after a while about the deaths of the characters.

The second major survey on the subject was undertaken in 1957, by author and teacher Edward Blishen, on behalf of the Council for Children's Welfare. For a fortnight, 700 parents monitored their children's television watching and produced written reports about it. Much of what was said reflects precisely the same fears that parents are currently expressing about 'screen time' and the use of electronic media. One mother said that, 'They don't want to go to the Scouts or any other movement because there is always something they want to watch.' Another remarked that her child, 'Had four books for Christmas and hasn't read them yet.'

Even more interesting was what the parents had to say about violence on television. Ask any baby boomer about television programmes that they enjoyed in the 1950s and almost without exception, they will mention, among others, the Western series that were so popular at that time, *The Lone Ranger*, *Gunsmoke*, *Maverick* and so on. Viewing these programmes on black-and-white televisions is remembered as being a charming, family pursuit, far removed from the images to which children are routinely exposed these days on the Internet or in computer games such as *Grand Theft Auto*. But Edward Blishen was under no illusions about the matter when he announced in November 1957 the result of his investigations into children's viewing habits and their parents; opinions on what they were watching. He told a meeting called by the Council for Children's Welfare that parents had used words like 'nasty', 'alien', 'frightening' and 'terror-making' to describe what they had seen when watching children's programmes. He went on to say that the objection of most parents was to the great amount of Wild West violence.

It is odd to think now that people sixty years ago were seriously concerned about the effect on children of watching *The Lone Ranger*! Nevertheless, Westerns like that were causing the greatest uneasiness among parents, who were afraid that not only were their children being conditioned to accept as unremarkable the death by shooting or stabbing each week of various people on the screen, but also that there was the risk that some children would go on to copy the kind of thing they were shown week after week. We remember at this point that the Walt Disney *Davy Crockett* television series, which was tremendously popular among many children in the 1950s, was blamed by doctors for eye injuries caused by children firing bows and arrows or airguns at each other. The dangers of children copying what they saw on television Westerns was far from being a theoretical one: it led to many children each year losing their eyes.

In short, both professionals and parents in the 1950s were starting to feel that there might be serious disadvantages for children spending too much time gazing at screens. It caused them to get less exercise and to disengage from the real world, living vicariously through the characters they saw on the screen. It was also responsible for a decline in the reading of books and harming education by preventing or discouraging schoolchildren from doing their homework in the evening. The idea was also being increasingly voiced that it was not good for children to be watching so many violent deaths every evening and that some vulnerable children might be impelled to copy the actions of actors whom they saw stabbing or shooting people. American Westerns and detective series were thought to be especially suspect in this respect.

It is not hard to see strong similarities between the fears voiced in the 1950s about the damaging effects of television-watching on children and the modern anxiety that using the Internet or playing violent computer games is causing harm to growing minds. Let's look at what else was being said on this subject and then compare it with some of the concerns currently being expressed about electronic media.

Throughout the 1950s, there had been increasing fears, not just in Britain but also in the United States, that a diet of violence in the form of Westerns and police shows was not good for children and might either desensitise them to violence generally or even incite them to commit acts of violence themselves. The *Manchester Guardian* had no doubt at all about this and in an editorial on 1 April 1960, they set out the case as they saw it without mincing words. Beginning uncompromisingly, by saying that, 'Violence and brutality on television present a special problem', the writer went on to detail the harm done by the relatively new mass medium of television: 'Even if, as it is fashionable to suggest today, shooting, knifing and many forms of sudden death are accepted merely as a form of stylised fantasy, without relation to life, the long-term effect of a diet of violence and brutality can only be harmful. Those who sup on murder may come to think it a normal meal.' Strange to think that popular programmes of the 1950s could possibly be thought of in this way. Could watching *Perry Mason* or *77 Sunset Strip* really have been harmful to the baby boomers?

We saw in a previous chapter that the video of *Child's Play 3: Chucky's Revenge* was thought by some newspapers to be implicated in the murder of a toddler, in much the same way that Iris Dawkins' death in 1960 had been linked to television-watching. Once computer games became popular, they too were blamed for encouraging murder. In July 2004, 17-year-old Warren Leblanc pleaded guilty to the murder of a 14-year-old boy. Leblanc had been an enthusiastic player of the Playstation game *Manhunt* and it was widely claimed in the press that the game had precipitated the murder itself, the *Daily Mirror* carrying a headline which proclaimed, 'Obsessed teen guilty of brutal copycat murder'.

The fear of what watching violence on television might lead children and young people to get up to, grew after 1960, until on 29 March 1962 Home Secretary Richard Austen Butler, known affectionately as 'Rab', announced the setting up of an enquiry into the effects of television on young people. The catalyst for this move was the furore about a graphic portrayal of a murder during a BBC production of Charles Dickens' *Oliver Twist*. This resulted in so many protests that the Postmaster-General, Reginald Bevins, was obliged to make a statement to the House of Commons. He described the scene in the television adaptation, which showed Bill Sykes killing Nancy, as 'brutal and inexcusable'. What caused particular outrage was that this had been a children's programme, broadcast at 5 pm on a Sunday afternoon.

We should perhaps stop here and think about what an extraordinary situation we are witnessing. It is a common lament among older people that families all sitting down to watch the same television programme is very much a thing of the past. Parents will instead watch one thing, while their children are in different rooms viewing catch-up TV or some film streamed from the Internet. One hears parents talk of the days when they were themselves teenagers and the whole family would be watching some favourite programme in each other's company, a popular sitcom, perhaps. It is also thought by many parents that both the quality and content of much of what their children are viewing leaves something to be desired.

With all this in mind, it is almost beyond belief to see what the reactions were sixty years ago to things like *Davy Crockett* and *The Lone Ranger*, or even BBC adaptations of novels by Charles Dickens. This was all radical and alarming stuff in the late 1950s and early 1960s and thought to pose threats to the psychological health of vulnerable children. How happy we would be today if our children wished to watch a television version of *Oliver Twist* with us! In 1962, though, it was enough to cause the Home Secretary to launch a government enquiry. Television programmes of this sort were honestly believed to be as bad as anything which our own children and grandchildren are now accessing on the Internet.

There was among both ordinary parents and also many professionals a fear that television was responsible if not for actually causing violence and deaths, then at least exacerbating problems among children. In some instances, violent images seen by children on television were directly blamed for subsequent deaths. In August 1963, the inquest was held in East London of an 11-year-old boy called Russell Sudbury. He had died of hanging at his home in Hainault. The dead boy had been found by his uncle, James Banks, who gave evidence at the inquest. Mr Banks had no doubt at all what had been responsible for his nephew's death and after telling the court of how he had given the child the 'kiss of life', in a vain attempt to revive him, he continued, 'I understand he had seen a television drama in which –', but was swiftly interrupted by the Coroner, Mr Kenshole.

Because of the controversy surrounding the possible role of television in promoting violent or dangerous behaviour, the Coroner investigating the death of Russell Sudbury devoted some time to trying to dampen down speculation about whether television could be blamed for the boy's death. He said;

> There's no lesson we can learn from this because it's quite impossible to say, 'Little boys should not be allowed to play with ropes.' You can't stop them, even if you want to. I don't think you should bother too much about whether he learned this by watching television, it's quite impossible to come to a conclusion. I have my doubts as to whether television did, in fact, play any part in this. This is an idea about which coroners' views have been sought as to whether violence or death, as in this case, in youngsters is brought about as a result of what they see on television.

Still, not all children at that time were slumped on the sofa, staring vacantly at the TV screen. One medium which was hugely popular in the years at which we are looking was comics. Reading of course played an integral part in the enjoyment of comics, some of which were actually educational. Many baby boomers, especially those from middle-class homes, have very strong memories of magazines like *Look and Learn*. Show some 60-year-olds an old copy of *Look and Learn* and they are likely to declare roundly that modern children would not have the patience to read something like this, with its informative articles on everything under the sun, from how radar works to the history of the Roman Empire. The early issues of this children's magazine, which began publication in 1962, had a weekly circulation of a million copies. It is hard to imagine such a magazine being as popular these days. Could this be evidence that children fifty-five years ago were more curious about the world and had the staying power to read quite complicated articles about pretty obscure and complex subjects?

Strange to say, there was very strong opposition throughout the 1950s and 1960s by many teachers and not a few parents to the reading of comics, which were believed to harm children mentally in a number of ways, not least by making them unable to focus on and absorb longer printed texts. There was a widespread feeling that the reading of comics tended to shorten children's attention-spans and harm their vocabulary, some of the worries that we currently have in fact about textspeak and the use of tablets. The captions and speech bubbles in comics were usually composed of simple, short words and some people worried that this did not stretch a child's ability to read. Comics were discouraged at school and forbidden in many middle-class homes. Even so-called 'educational' comics such as *Look and Learn* were frowned upon by a lot of teachers. It was not only educational considerations which were causing alarm, however; other, and graver, fears were being expressed at that time about comics.

Comics for children were a relatively new medium in the 1950s and although they are now remembered favourably as just one more of those relics from a gentler time, they were felt then by many professionals to be undesirable and even dangerous. There had been story papers for children for many years; things like the *Magnet*, which of course introduced Billy Bunter to the world. In the early 1920s and early 1930s, new magazines for children came along. *Hotspur* and *Wizard* carried exciting and fantastic serials for boys. Although illustrated with the occasional picture, these papers consisted of pages covered with densely printed text. True, they were sometimes dismissed as trashy in content but it was undeniable that children were actually *reading* when they leafed through *Hotspur* and the content of the stories was largely unobjectionable.

All this changed just before the beginning of the Second World War when comics as we now understand them appeared on the market simultaneously in Britain and America. There had been much earlier incarnations of the format, *Comic Cuts* having been published as earlier as 1890, but children's comics as we know them really began circulating in the 1930s. In June 1938, Superman made his debut in America in the first edition of *Action Comics*. The following month saw the publication of what would become one of the most popular British comics, the *Beano* which introduced Lord Snooty and his pals to the world. The very different characters of Superman and Lord Snooty thus appeared for the first time within weeks of each other. The previous year had seen the first issues of *Dandy* in Britain and *Detective Comics* in America, the comic in which Batman was first featured in 1939.

It is difficult in retrospect to understand what a menace comics were thought to be to the baby boomers in the 1950s and 1960s. Today, we see them as representing all that was harmless and good about childhood at that time. The idea that comics featuring Superman and Lord Snooty could have been seen as subversive, insidiously promoting homosexuality, damaging to education and likely to incite crime and disorder must seem vanishingly unlikely to modern readers! Never the less, concern about comics and their effects upon children and young people began in the United States and spread to this country, resulting eventually in yet another moral panic which led to a hastily-enacted piece of legislation aimed at tackling what came to be seen as a terrible scourge.

Before looking in detail at what was being said about comics in the 1950s, it might be useful to look both backwards and forwards at other media which were believed at one time to pose a threat to children. We saw that the cinema was thought in the years following the end of the First World War to be implicated in the decline of children's use of public lending libraries. It was also said that some children were so addicted to this form of entertainment that they would steal money to ensure that they could visit the cinema as often as they wished. There was talk too of children copying what was seen on the screen and committing criminal acts based upon what characters in the films were doing.

Fast-forward eighty years and we see similar concerns being voiced about 'video nasties' and their bad influence on children, even, as in the case of the James Bulger murder, apparently being associated with crimes of extreme violence. Computer games and the Internet are also spoken of by some older adults in the same terms. All these worries and anxieties are essentially a consequence of adults fretting about new media which were not around when they were themselves youngsters. Today, the baby boomers are alarmed at the use of computers and tablets because they did not have such things as this when they were children and cannot imagine that a childhood centred around electronic gadgets can possibly be healthy or fulfilling, so they hunt around for bad things which they can blame on what they do not fully understand. Thus we see a head teacher criticising the use of tablets and claiming that they are preventing children from being able to write properly or even climb trees. What the baby boomers have quite forgotten is that their own childhood amusements were the subject of just this kind of uninformed attack by adults. Far from being a fairly unobjectionable way for children to pass some of their leisure time, both watching Western series on black-and-white televisions and reading Superman comics were widely believed at one time to be incredibly damaging to developing minds.

In 1954 a book was published in America which summed up the fears that many parents and teachers had about the new medium of children's comics. Comics, in the accepted modern format, had only been around for fifteen years or so and thus qualified as a modern phenomenon. *Seduction of the Innocent*, by psychiatrist Frederic Wertham, set out on its cover the theme which Wertham expounded in the book, 'the influence of comic books on today's youth'. Wertham was not concerned with this or that type of comic: he condemned them all wholesale, even Superman, whom he described as a Fascist, and Batman, who was, according to Wertham, enjoying a flagrantly open gay relationship with his young ward Robin.

Reading through *Seduction of the Innocent* today is an eerie experience, for the entire thesis could have been taken from a modern newspaper denouncing the perils and ill effects of the Internet on children. The main thrust of Wertham's argument was that repeatedly seeing images in comics could cause children to view such behaviour or events as being somehow normal. This was, he suggested, a major cause of juvenile delinquency. Attention was also drawn in the book to the fact that scenes of violence were accompanied by advertisements for air rifles and knives. It was according to Frederic Wertham, as though those producing the comic were setting out to promote anti-social behaviour. We must remember that British comics too carried advertisements for airguns, to which nobody at the time took exception.

In addition to his denunciation of superhero comics (Wonder Woman was clearly a lesbian according to Wertham), the genre known colloquially as 'horror comics' came in for condemnation, featuring as they did scenes of graphic violence and gore. If Batman contributed to children becoming confused about family structure and Superman caused them to embrace 'Un-American' attitudes, then it was the horror comics which made sex maniacs and violent criminals of them. This particular type of comic gave rise to one of the greatest moral panics involving children in 1950s Britain. These so-called horror comics were being imported from the United States in the years following the end of the war and after *Seduction of the Innocent* became famous, a campaign started in Britain to stamp out the dangerous new publications.

In November 1954 the National Union of Teachers staged an exhibition in London of what they considered to be some of the more harmful material being circulated. A reporter from the *Manchester Guardian* went along and reported on what he saw there: 'Skeletons embracing young women, scaly monsters doing appalling things to brunettes in tight dresses and barely clad target girls – ringed by knives – watching the approach of axes thrown by blue hands. There is a morbid preoccupation with death and rotting corpses . . .' Truly the video nasties of the time! On a nearby table were placed copies of comics which the NUT regarded as being harmless: *Beano, Dandy, Eagle* and so on.

The one question about which everybody seemed a little vague was what harm these comics showing skeletons and murderers actually caused to children. Reporters were told that: 'Statistics painstakingly acquired over several years by a master in a secondary modern boys' school show that bright children soon become bored by horror comics and reject them. But the less intelligent are more susceptible and read them over a much longer period – this is the danger.' From this reading of the situation, the danger appeared to be simply that unintelligent boys would waste their time reading these comics, but why that would be a bad thing was not at all clear to anybody.

It is in the nature though of moral panics that reason tends to go out of the window as everybody gets caught up in the rush to condemn whatever it is that is threatening society. It was the same with horror comics. Whether action should be taken by the government or on the other hand if parents should take the initiative, the plain fact was that millions of these comics were floating around and something had to be done about them. On 21 October Mrs C. Frankenburg, a magistrate and social worker, warned that urgent action was now needed and that parents had a duty to see that their children were not reading horror comics. She claimed that 60 million copies of such comics were being sold each year in Britain. Once again, the actual danger from all these comics about skeletons, murders and so on was not made clear. A few weeks later, the Archbishop of Canterbury had a meeting with Home Secretary Lloyd George, during which he talked of the strong public feeling aroused by horror comics.

Once the Archbishop of Canterbury had joined the fray, it was only a matter of time before legislation was framed which would protect children from American comics. The Children and Young Persons (Harmful Publications) Bill was duly drawn up and by the early spring of the following year was making its way through Parliament. There was much debate about the best way to define a horror comic and at one point it looked as though newspapers too would be included within the scope of the bill. Common sense prevailed and the possibility of press censorship sank into oblivion. Prosecutions under the act were rare and within a year or two, everybody had forgotten all about the fuss.

Despite all the hysteria about imported horror comics, the primary objection to comics in Britain had always been educational, rather than moral. It was perfectly possible to follow the stories in the strip cartoons without reading any of the words and this was, according to some teachers, a disincentive to the acquisition of literacy. If a child could leaf through a comic and make sense of it without being able to understand a single word, might he or she be content to remain at this level of restricted understanding and not feel any need to learn to read? The vocabulary of the average comic was in any case meagre and they could not really be said to stretch children's comprehension. It was also claimed that children in comics tended to be aggressive, sneaky and prone to disregarding the authority of parents and teachers. The Bash Street Kids, who appeared in the same year that the nation was in a frenzy about horror comics, might be setting a bad example to the nation's youth.

The chief problem was seen to be that if children spent all their time staring at rubbishy comics, then they might never get round to reading real books and would be intellectually impoverished as a consequence. What if they never grew out of the *Beano* and felt the need to move on to more challenging fare? It was an alarming prospect, but there is no evidence that this fate ever befell any children as they were growing up. The visceral dislike felt by many educated professionals for comics extended to educational material presented in the format of a comic. Even a general-knowledge magazine, beloved of middle-class baby boomers and their families, did not escape censure.

In 1962, a new magazine for children began publication. The cover was brightly coloured and inside were illustrated articles on everything from the Grand Canyon to the life of Vincent Van Gogh. The humorous classic *Three Men in a Boat* began to be serialized in that first issue as well. Some fifty-five years later, *Look and Learn* is still spoken of with reverence as an illustration from the distant past showing just how things have gone downhill intellectually for children since those days. Let us see what educationalists were saying about *Look and Learn* at the time though.

In October 1965, the Advisory Centre for Education in London published an analysis of educational comics which were available for children. They were scathing about all of them. A panel consisting of a college lecturer in English, a scientist and an illustrator examined two issues of each of the educational comics on the market at that time: *Elizabethan*, *Treasure*, *Wonderland*, *The New English Encyclopaedia* and of course *Look and Learn*. The members of the panel ferociously denounced every one of these supposedly educational comics. There were individual criticisms of each comic, but a general disapproval of the very idea of comics permeated their judgements. Comics, they said, could never replace or even compare to 'that primary material which lies in books and provides imaginative nourishment and enlargement of the mind'. The panel went on to say that none of the comics examined offered, 'a single area of experience which is within the capacity of any good book, whether a legend of King Arthur or a biography of Freud'. Of *Elizabethan*, a magazine for teenagers, it was noted that there was an absence of sex and political discussion, which was 'surprising in a magazine for this age range'. Similarly sharp remarks were made about the other comics.

In view of the affectionate regard in which *Look and Learn* is now held by older adults, it is fascinating to read the criticisms made by professionals at the height of its popularity. '*Look and Learn,*' we are informed, was printed on 'rather poor paper, with a number of crudely-drawn illustrations and a cramped presentation of material'. The report went on to say that although plenty of colour was used in the pictures, the overall effect was not good and much of the material did not seem particularly designed to appeal to children. A feature on mercury was said to be the worst scientific article the panel had ever seen.

The overall conclusion of the three people commissioned by the Advisory Centre for Education was that nothing could compare with books for stimulating and informing children and that comics like *Look and Learn* were trashy and inferior substitutes for the real thing. All of which goes to show how standards change. These days, most parents would be thrilled if their children were to display as much interest in magazine articles on the Grand Canyon as they do in watching Youtube clips about kittens behaving cutely. However, times change and back in the 1960s reading *Look and Learn* was treated as a time-wasting activity which distracted children and prevented them from reading proper books or engaging with the real world.

According to the Spanish philosopher and essayist George Santayana, those who cannot remember the past are condemned to repeat it. The truth of this aphorism has been neatly illustrated in this chapter. The generation of young people who grew up after the First World War were thought be obsessed with visiting the cinema and no longer bothering to visit the local lending library because they had lost interest in reading. Their parents couldn't understand why they weren't content to visit the music hall or read 'Penny Dreadfuls', the things which had satisfied them when they were themselves young. The young cinema-goers of the early 1920s went on in turn to criticize their own children, the baby boomers, for wanting to watch television and waste their time reading comics.

When they grew up and became parents and grandparents themselves, one might have thought that the baby boomers would remember all this and adopt a slightly more laid-back attitude to the latest media to be denounced for harming children; things such as video nasties, violent computer games and sexual imagery on the Internet. Instead, the baby boomers follow dutifully in their own parents' footsteps and bemoan the fact that children today can't be satisfied with watching *Dixon of Dock Green* on the television or curling up with a copy of *Eagle* or *Look and Learn*! It is amusing to speculate what new entertainments today's young people will find to criticize their own children for enjoying. One thing is quite certain and that is that is that we have not yet reached the end of the road in this particular cycle of human behaviour. From Socrates complaining about written language to William Tyndale and his disapproval of the 'filthy' printed chapbooks which were corrupting children in the early sixteenth century, all the way to the evil effects of novels on Victorian girls; current worries about online porn and so on are just the latest manifestation of an extremely ancient tendency for older generations to find fault with those who are much younger.

Chapter 8

From *Janet and John* to *The Famous Five*:
Baby Boomer Childhood in Fiction

When reading children's books written for or enjoyed by baby boomer children, one is struck by something very curious; that almost every one of the children who feature in children's books which were popular in those days attended private schools, most of which are boarding schools. Whether we look at Enid Blyton's *Famous Five* books, the Narnia stories of C. S. Lewis, the William books written by Richmal Crompton, Jennings, Molesworth or any of the other children's books popular at that time; the picture is the same. All except for William went to fee-paying boarding schools. William attended a private school: his father complains at times of the amount of money which his son's education is costing him. There must be something inherently attractive to children about the idea of boarding schools, because of course the latest and most spectacularly successful children's books, those featuring Harry Potter, are also set in an establishment of this kind.

One point which stands out when looking at the children's books of this period is the more or less complete absence of parents. This may well have a bearing on the feelings of adults who grew up at that time, that children being out and about by themselves was in the first place quite normal and secondly perfectly safe. It is almost as though they had been indoctrinated into this strange and counterintuitive point of view from a very early age by the books which they read. If so, then this brainwashing began very young, and was given almost, as one might say, with their mother's milk or, at the very least, when they started school and first acquired the rudiments of literacy.

The very first baby boomers, those who began school in 1950 or 1951, learned to read from a new reading-scheme which was published in 1949; the *Janet and John* books. These, the first books which many children ever encountered, set the tone for much of the subsequent reading in childhood. They were attractive, with full-page coloured illustrations following the adventures of the eponymous children as they explored the world. There was something enchanting about the *Janet and John* books, and they were not at all like previous and generally dull reading-schemes which had been many children's first encounter with the acquisition of literacy until the 1950s. In a sense, *Janet and John* reflected the lives which the baby boomers would experience as they grew up.

The *Janet and John* books show a world which the baby boomers came to think of as the natural order of things; which is to say small children wandering around in hazardous circumstances without any adults to protect them from harm. Looking at *Here We Go*, the first book in the series, we are at once confronted with the question of where the action is taking place. The children seemingly live in some sylvan paradise, neither town nor country. There is no sign of any habitation, nor yet of farmland. A bridge is visible in one picture, which might suggest a park, except that everything is a little too wild for that. The two children can be no more than four or five and yet they are quite alone in this place. A river and lake are featured and both children get in the water and start larking about. John climbs up a willow tree with the evident intention of leaping into the water. We are left with the impression that it is OK for children of kindergarten age to be playing in deep water by themselves, without any parental supervision. In later books, we see the two small children on a bridge over a railway, with John pulling himself onto the parapet in a most hazardous fashion, just as a steam train is approaching. There are no adults in sight. They also wander round an airfield, also unaccompanied. As far as can be made out, these children are at large in the world with nobody at all keeping an eye on them.

It looks very much as though the normalization of young children being out and about without adults was being pushed from the first days at school, with books like *Janet and John* portraying it as being the most natural thing in the world for little boys and girls to be jumping into wide rivers or climbing up onto railway bridges whenever they felt like it. Needless to say, there were never any unpleasant consequences when Janet and John run about on heaps of jagged boulders, play with a dog, climb trees or stand up to their necks in flowing water. What could possibly go wrong? They certainly don't get abducted by child molesters, run over by trains or end up catching polio from the contaminated water in which they are playing!

It has to be suspected that the literature which baby boomers read when young went a good way towards encouraging them in the notion that children would be fine if they were to be wholly separated from their parents and left to their own devices. After the *Janet and John* books, we see the theme enlarged upon, as children grow a little older, in various Ladybird books. Here, we see the Golden Age of baby boomer childhood in all its glory. There can be no doubt that these books both showed how children lived during the 1950s and 1960s and also, by implication, endorsed the lifestyle. They may not inaptly be said to be both descriptive and prescriptive, portraying a happy world in which children go about by themselves as a matter of course. In 2007, a compilation of images and text from Ladybird books was published, a celebration of both the books and the childhood which they depicted. Various celebrities such as Alan Titchmarsh and Tony Robinson contributed essays, talking of their early lives and what Ladybird books had meant to them. The introduction to this book, *Boys and Girls; A Ladybird Book of Childhood*, explicitly and unashamedly plugged the myth of baby boomer childhood. Headed *A Golden Age*, it begins, '*Boys and Girls* is a celebration of childhood – a golden age of childhood...' Leafing through the *Ladybird Book of Childhood* is a fascinating experience; particularly for those who were around when the images first appeared in print. Tony Robinson illustrated his own essay with pictures from the Ladybird book *The Party*, published in 1960. One of the pictures shows two children, brother and sister, walking to a birthday party to which they have been invited. The boy and girl can be no more than five or six and yet we see them making their way along a long, deserted suburban street. It would have been a common enough scene then: today it looks like a case of criminal neglect! It is precisely the same as the *Janet and John* books: little boys and girls out and about without anybody to take care of them. Elsewhere in the book we see two children aged perhaps seven or eight, being helped onto a bus by a cheerful and smiling conductor. They too are out by themselves. This too would have been perfectly normal in 1960.

Once again, just as with the *Janet and John* books, we ask ourselves whether or not this is a case of art imitating life or the other way round. Did these constant images to which children and parents were exposed have the effect of leading them to believe that it was natural and safe for children to wander the streets alone? It may have been convenient for mothers to turf the children out during washday, so that they could get on with a long and difficult task without the kids under their feet, but surely at the back of their minds they must have realized that sending five-year-olds out to play by themselves was not really a good idea? Perhaps seeing the smiling, happy children in the Ladybird books and so on lulled them into a false sense of security.

In the *Famous Five* books, by Enid Blyton, are children, the oldest of whom is just 12 years of age, who travel in horse-drawn caravans, go to sea in a dingy, tackle spies and robbers, outwit the police and generally carry on in a way which would leave most adults feeling a little nervous. We see here the tradition at which we have already looked, of the older child being left in charge of younger siblings. Julian is 12 and yet he assumes complete responsibility for three younger children, his own brother and sister and also a cousin. This arrangement was of course calculated to strike a chord with child readers of the time, many 12-year-olds would have had similar experiences, if not in such exotic circumstances.

It is hard to overestimate the influence of books such as the *Famous Five* on the children growing up in the 1950s and 1960s. As adults, their frequently-expressed views that children should be allowed to walk to school alone and visit parks by themselves are shaped by such fantasies. They were not told of the horrific numbers of children killed by cars, nor of those who had died from other accidents or been abducted, abused and even murdered. In all the books which they read, from *Janet and John* onwards, nothing bad ever befell children out on their own. Of course, sometimes Julian, Dick, Ann and George might be kidnapped by crooks or locked in a cellar or dungeon, but their resourcefulness always enable them to resolve such minor difficulties.

The subliminal messages from *Janet and John* and the *Famous Five* were reinforced by such classic children's literature as *The Lion, the Witch and the Wardrobe* and *Prince Caspian*. Here too are children whose parents are never in evidence. They are packed off first to a remote country house and then to a boarding school; we never see or hear from their mothers and fathers. They too roam the world, in this case an alien one, never coming to any harm. They fight wolves, face wicked enchantresses, engage usurping kings in hand-to-hand combat and yet always come out on top. Once again, the message is clear: older children may be safely left in charge of young siblings and whatever the perils they may face, it will all end well.

Of course, another view of the case might simply be that these books are wish-fulfilment and that by creating a world free of adult interference, the authors are really appealing to their readers' deepest desires. Imagine, they are saying, a world where you are never sent to bed at a particular time and may explore wherever you please without anything bad happening to you. Could this also be the reason that boarding schools are such a popular setting for children's books; that it frees the protagonists from the interference of parents? This might be persuasive if it were not for the fact that throughout the baby boomers' childhood years, they *were* as a matter of course allowed to leave the house unescorted from an astonishingly early age, as young as three or four, and very often were left all day in the care of children who might themselves be only 11 or 12. This part of the plots of these books was not make-believe, but reflected what was widely seen as acceptable neglect by parents. From this perspective, the William stories of Richmal Crompton are very interesting.

The William books were tremendously popular with baby boomers, the last of them being published in 1970, a year or two after Richmal Crompton's death. The later books deal with such things as television, pop stars and space exploration. Despite coming from a thoroughly respectable and stable home background, William and his gang present as what we would today describe as 'feral' children. Chronic underachievers academically, they roam the streets and countryside aimlessly, causing all sorts of trouble for ordinary people. They trespass, smash windows, break into empty houses and fight rival gangs with air rifles, bows and arrows and catapults. William always carried a knife with him. There was nothing in the slightest outlandish or improbable about the way of life led by William and his friends; it was because it was so familiar to readers that the books became so wildly popular. William was certainly a lot more unruly and destructive than the characters of whom Enid Blyton wrote, but there is a common thread running through both the William books and those featuring the Famous Five, which was that children could cope perfectly well if left to their own devices and no matter what befell them, they would always arrive home safely by teatime. Arriving home in time for tea, after many vicissitudes, is a regular event in the William stories. In neither Richmal Crompton's works, nor those of Enid Blyton, do any of the children suffer anything worse than a grazed knee or, at worst, a black eye. They certainly do not lose fingers or eyes from playing with fireworks or being shot at with airguns, both, as we have seen, genuine risks for children in the real world at that time.

It is difficult to avoid the suspicion that the books that they read as children have somehow become mixed up in the minds of the now grown-up baby boomers with their actual childhood experiences, and that much of the golden age of which they dream has really been taken from the pages of the stories with which they grew up. This might account, at least in part, for the constant refrain of 'back in time for tea'. Whether it is William and his friends who are charging round the neighbourhood damaging gardens and breaking windows or the characters from the Narnia books, fighting witches and wolves, the recurring theme is that no harm will come to children when they are having adventures on their own with no adults to protect them. Some of this attitude must subconsciously have rubbed off on the children reading these stories. How else are we able to explain the repeated and untruthful assurances of those who grew up at that time that everything was safer in those days and that no children ever came to any serious harm?

The world portrayed in children's fiction of the 1950s bears a startling and uncanny similarity to that which we see in modern newspaper articles about that period. As we have seen, there is a stark dissonance between the generally accepted image of childhood at that time and the reality for most children. The image of happy, healthy childhood to which so many subscribe is not drawn from reality, but is a compendium of many misleading or false memories from five or six decades ago. We see 12-year-old Julian in the *Famous Five* books, cheerfully taking care of his younger sister Ann, while scarcely catching a glimpse of their parents, who are content to leave the welfare of their two younger children to a 12-year-old. In books by Enid Blyton, of course, this sets the stage for all manner of fantastic and exciting adventures. In real life children like Julian were always being used in this way as convenient babysitters and childminders, but with less satisfactory results than those seen in story books. We remember the police inspector in Manchester in 1961, who told reporters that some of those being allowed to trespass on railway lines were toddlers. This was the reality of letting older children care for young brothers and sisters.

If we want to study works of fiction which shed the clearest light on the behaviour of children in the 1950s when there were no adults around to monitor or moderate their conduct, then two books stand out. Both were published in the early 1950s, just three years apart. The first of these is perhaps Enid Blyton's least-known book, *The Six Bad Boys*. In it, Blyton abandons her habitual practice of showing how children can traipse about without adults, with things never going too badly wrong, and shows how children playing out sometimes end up running wild and getting into serious trouble with the police. *The Six Bad Boys* focuses on the lives of three middle-class families, two of which have no fathers to control their children. They are in fact what was once known as 'broken homes'. Bob's father is dead and Tom's leaves home after a series of rows with his mother. The two boys team up together and eventually join a street gang who steal money from a newsagent, among other things. The strength of the book lies in its depiction of the perils of 'playing out' and shows vividly how the aimless hanging round the streets could result in dangerous or criminal activity. Here are Tom and Bob 'playing out' when it begins to rain and they do not want to go home:

> 'What shall we do?' said Bob. 'We can't mess about in the rain. I was rather thinking going down to the canal and getting on board a barge that's lying there. Nobody's on it. We could have explored a bit.'
>
> 'Well we can't now that it's pouring with rain,' said Tom. 'But I don't particularly want to go back home, do you?'
>
> 'No,' said Bob, decidedly
>
> 'Got any money?' said Tom. 'We could go to the cinema. There's a good picture on.'
>
> 'I've only a penny or two,' said Bob. 'It *would* be nice to go to the cinema. It's warm in there, and you can forget everything except the picture.

In the end, the boys get into a cinema free, through the fire exit, and get into trouble. This begins a downwards spiral, which leads them to the juvenile court. The scenes showing the boys trying to amuse themselves when they have no money are exquisitely drawn and very unlike Enid Blyton's other work, in which playing out is shown to be one long lark.

Although not written for children, *Lord of the Flies* describes perfectly just how things become when there are no grown-ups about to step in and take charge. Children, especially boys, can be unbelievably callous and cruel. It is only a step or two from pulling the wings off flies to mistreating smaller children. The savagery that is to be found in *Lord of the Flies* does not seem at all over the top to anybody who played on bomb sites about the time that the novel was written. In the book a party of English schoolboys of 11 and 12 are stranded on a desert island. Just as happened regularly in the early 1950s, when the book was being written, with no adults to check their behaviour or step in when things get out of hand, the descent into barbarism is swift, as survival of the fittest and most ruthless becomes the order of the day. Similar scenes were played out in real life every day at the time that William Golding was writing this novel. It was only the fact that the children had to be back in time for tea which stopped the wanton violence, cruelty and bullying from reaching the logical and inevitable conclusion so graphically described in *Lord of the Flies*. The assaults on young and vulnerable children by those older and stronger, at which we have looked, show that the conduct of the schoolboys in this book is anything but improbable, once adults are removed from the picture.

Chapter 9

Limited Choices:
How Much Freedom Did the Baby Boomers Actually Have as Children?

It is frequently and firmly asserted that children in twenty-first-century Britain have less freedom than those of previous generations. Expressions such as 'helicopter parenting' have been coined to describe mothers and fathers who cannot just leave children to their own devices, but instead strive ceaselessly to ensure that every minute of their offspring's lives are filled with enriching and educative activities. Like helicopters, such parents hover above their children, supervising their leisure time, arranging music lessons and even selecting friends for them. It is for most of us axiomatic that such suffocatingly close involvement in a child's life must stifle their independence. It is certainly a very different style of parenting from the *laissez faire* ways which so many baby boomers remember.

On every side, regret is expressed that children cannot be given the freedom that their parents and grandparents evidently enjoyed so much. Adults talk in fulsome terms about their own carefree childhoods, while at the same time explaining regretfully that such a lifestyle is no longer possible. Let us consider, before going any further, just what we mean in this context by the word 'freedom'. Freedom, if it means anything at all, must surely entail the ability to make choices; to decide upon one course of action over another. Perhaps thinking in this way will show what choices children in the 1950s and 1960s faced in their lives; how much freedom they actually enjoyed.

Imagine for a moment that you are a 12-year-old child in a house with no machinery or gadgets at all run by electricity, other than the lights and perhaps a mains-operated Bakelite radio. For amusement, you have a few books which you have read time and again, some dolls, marbles, a lump of plasticene and possibly one or two board games like snakes and ladders or ludo. Your mother and father are frequently too busy to give you any attention and there is no telephone in the house, no way at all of connecting with anybody in the world other than those present in the house at that moment. There is no money available to go to the cinema or visit a café. You have literally nothing to do. Really, there is only one choice to be made: staying indoors, bored to tears, or leaving the house and hoping to bump into some school friends. Once you have met friends, none of whom are likely to have any money, the only things to do will be play in the park or perhaps go and stand on a windy platform at a railway station and write down the details of passing trains in an old exercise book. Put in those terms, the baby boomer child was distinctly short of choices. The pastimes of that period about which everybody now speaks with such pleasure, playing Cowboys and Indians or trainspotting, were not a sign of increased freedom at all, but rather the precise opposite; the symptom of an almost complete lack of choice on the part of the children growing up at that time.

Let's pretend that we can now offer the bored child, trapped in the house with nothing to do, some real freedom, in the form of a few more choices. Suppose we told him or her that there was the chance of watching the latest Disney film, in colour, in the comfort of a warm bedroom? What if we suggested the possibility that instead of being obliged to trek round to people's houses in order to speak to them, one could instead chat endlessly on a telephone which also featured live colour television pictures of the person to whom one was speaking? Or suppose that we gave such a child the opportunity to visit a warm, bright, indoor shopping mall, and being given enough money to eat and drink in a café where friends also hung out? It cannot be doubted for a moment that our hypothetical 1950s child would leap at such new choices, which would be vastly more attractive than the meagre opportunities for entertainment and stimulation that were usually available. Who wouldn't choose to do some of the things that are there for today's children, rather than hang aimlessly about in a park or by a railway line? No wonder the children of that time used to get into such mischief; this is what is meant when adults today talk of 'making their own entertainment'.

From this perspective, modern children have infinitely more choices and therefore freedom, than their grandparents had at a similar age. Never in the history of British childhood has a generation been faced with such a dizzying array of choice in leisure-time activities. It is not that modern children are forbidden from joining church youth clubs or watching trains at the local station, it is more that there are so many more interesting things to occupy their time. It may well be true that they tend to be driven to and from school, whereas at one time they would have walked alone, but so what? Why on earth would anybody in his or her senses *choose* to walk, when a lift is being offered in a car? There is an increasing tendency for even secondary school pupils of 14 or 15 to be driven to school in the mornings by their mothers and collected in the afternoon. This is hardly a loss of freedom, however; the children concerned are generally only too happy to be delivered and picked up like this.

Let us offer a couple more choices to our hypothetical baby boomer child. It is a cold winter's morning and a 10-year-old is about to leave for school. He or she faces a walk of a mile or more, bare-legged in the wind and rain, to get to school. Would this child decline the opportunity to be driven to school in a warm car, in favour of trudging through the bleak streets in the company of other similarly miserable children? It is unlikely. Anybody who can actually remember those days must surely realize that if children at that time had had the freedom that modern children have, that is to say had a choice in the matter, very few would have wished to continue walking to school in all weathers.

Let's offer one final choice to our baby boomer child. Photography was a very expensive hobby in the 1950s: even taking black-and-white pictures with a box camera bought at a jumble sale cost more than many families could afford. Few parents had enough money to spare to give cameras to their children and pay for them to have films developed regularly. As for the recording of sound or the taking of moving pictures, this would have been unheard of. What if we told a child from the 1950s that instead of playing Cowboys and Indians in a cold park, he or she could now take as many colour photographs as wished and even make films with a soundtrack? How many would have chosen to carry on hanging out in the park?

The lifestyle of British baby boomers as children was dictated by their economic circumstances and the technological developments of the era. Rather than being a time of unlimited choice and exhilarating freedom, those children's horizons were more cramped and restricted than can readily be imagined today. It was the very antithesis of freedom, if by freedom we do mean the ability to make choices.

This is one of the reasons that today's children and young people do not follow the way of life which their grandparents apparently found so enjoyable. They choose not to do so. Of course, parental anxieties are at work too today, in that many mothers and fathers are afraid that their children will come to harm if left alone in public. This is curious. A little investigation would soon reveal to anybody even remotely interested in the subject that children are at no more risk today from sudden death or abduction by sexual predators than they would have been in 1950, 1960 or 1970. If their parents are really convinced that their own childhoods were so wonderful, why on earth don't they give their own children this priceless gift of early freedom? The answer is of course very simple.

When harassed and busy mothers in the 1960s sent nine-year-olds like Robert Elms off to travel round central London alone for the day, they knew perfectly well that this was not a sensible or wise course of action. They too, just like their children, had very little choice in the matter. There was so much housework to do and much of it would be more easily accomplished without a little boy hanging round the house and complaining of being bored. In the 1950s, it would be a very rare housewife and mother who would say to herself, 'Blow it! I'm going to forget the housework, let everything go to the Devil, and just play with my son.' Of course, mothers did do that on occasion, but they could not just let everything slide too often. Husbands in those days were apt to get a little tetchy if their shirts weren't ironed or tea on the table when they got in from work. The mothers, like their children, had fewer choices and far less freedom in those days than is now the case.

Our common sense tells us now that we would not give a nine-year-old child a travelcard and send him off to London for the day. It would not be safe and he would be exposed to all sorts of hazards and risks, ranging from crossing the road carelessly to being bullied or mistreated by older children or adults. There is also a small, but definite, chance that a child out and about by himself in this way will be abducted or even murdered. This is not because the world is a more wicked and dangerous place now than it was a few years ago: we have looked at the misfortunes which befell many children during the years that the baby boomers were growing up. It is more that we now have a greater number of choices as parents. Just as our children have more freedom, in the sense of more choices, so do we. We can let our children sit and play on laptops or tablets, we most of us have cars, so that we can choose to drive them to school instead of letting them walk, there is money available for them to go to holiday clubs or play schemes; our choices as parents are far more varied than they were fifty years ago.

In short, the real reason why modern parents do not let their children go out and about by themselves from an earlier age has nothing to do with any supposed change in the hazards and risks which beset them. It is because they know perfectly well on one level that it was not safe for them to be out so much without adults when they were younger and they know the dangers inherent in such a course of action. 'Playing out' was born of necessity, not desire. Now that it is no longer necessary to chuck the children out of the house so that mother can spend an entire day boiling up water, scrubbing clothes on a washboard and then putting them through the mangle, and there are also so many things to amuse children in their own homes, children do not show any inclination to go wandering off in this way.

All this leaves us with a puzzling question. The 'playing out' of the baby boomers was, in effect, thrust upon them and their families by force of circumstance and not an option freely chosen on its merit. Britain was not some demi-paradise sixty years ago, no matter what the baby boomers would now have us believe. Why then do many people younger than the baby boomers seem happy to go along with this misleading picture of the past? Instead of treating the reminiscences of older people with the proper level of caution, there appears to be an uncritical acceptance among many people, even those in their 20s and 30s, of this whole myth of the golden age of childhood. In the next, and final, chapter, I shall explore one possible explanation for this, enlarging upon an idea at which we have already looked briefly.

Afterword

In this book we have looked at the strange myth which has been sedulously propagated over the last few years by baby boomers about the idyllic nature of their childhood. That they should themselves half believe this nonsense is perfectly understandable: it is, after all, a delusion to which people in late middle or old age have fallen prey for the whole of recorded history! They persuade themselves that things were far better in their youth and that this modern world cannot hold a candle to the times in which they grew up. What is a puzzling at first sight though, is why so many younger people, who were not even born in the 1950s and 1960s, should go along with all this. This requires a little explanation. The natural reaction of men and women in their 20s and 30s to their grandparents' tales about the enchanted realm in which they dwelt as children should be frank disbelief. We certainly don't expect younger adults to take these fairy stories at face value and start passing laws or formulating policies for health authorities based upon these old wives' tales!

When it is suggested that all schoolchildren should chant their times tables out loud, as was done in schools sixty years ago, those putting forward and arranging this scheme are not people in their 60s and 70s, but rather young professionals who grew up in the modern world. When a Chancellor of the Exchequer who wasn't born until 1971 introduces taxes on sugar which are aimed at slimming down children to the proportions they supposedly had in the 1950s, it is evident that he too has been persuaded that children's lives were genuinely better when the baby boomers were growing up. It looks as though the mania for the vanished world of the 1950s has begun with pensioners and then spread out and engulfed the nation.

There is an historical precedent for people in this country becoming possessed in this way of an affection for a mythical past era. This was the reaction among many artists, writers and intellectuals in mid-Victorian Britain to the Industrial Revolution. As the nineteenth century progressed, there was a widespread feeling that the pace of life was becoming intolerably fast, due largely to technological innovations. Steam trains and the telegraph were two very noticeable manifestations of this trend. For almost the whole of human history, the fastest way for people to travel and for information to be spread was either on foot or by means of a galloping horse. Now, somebody could be transported from one end of the country to another in a matter of hours and the transmission of news was, to all intents and purposes, instantaneous. When Victoria came to the throne in 1838, it took a month for information to reach England by ship from New York. By the 1870s, news was being carried over a transatlantic telegraph wire at the speed of light. For millennia, Britain had been an agrarian society, with labour following the rhythm of the seasons and the rising and setting of the sun. Now, every minute counted as people rushed to catch trains and hurried to be at the factory or office on time. Time was suddenly at a premium.

This change of pace was disturbing to older people and not universally attractive even to those who were younger. A distaste for the modern way of life grew; not only at the hectic speed with which things were now being done, but also at the commercial attitude which was the distinguishing mark of Victorian Britain. If only, it was thought, we could return to a simpler and gentler pastoral life, where things happened at a more leisurely rate and people were motivated by notions of justice and chivalry, rather than how quickly a profit could be made on this or that investment. A reaction to the perceived ugliness and mercantile values of the Industrial Revolution had been gathering momentum since the end of the eighteenth century. Gothic architecture had come into fashion, attempting to recreate the buildings of the Middle Ages in nineteenth-century civic and industrial buildings, ranging from railways stations to the Houses of Parliament. Artists and poets joined in with enthusiasm, depicting a sanitized and largely imaginary world of medieval heroism and love.

The royal family became caught up in the craze for the medieval, posing for paintings and statues which portrayed them as historical and semi-historical characters from the Middle Ages. Towards the end of the century William Morris and the Arts and Crafts movement emerged, deliberately opposing industrial production and championing cottage industries and individual craftsmen. The inspiration for much of the architecture, art and poetry associated with this trend was to be found in Sir Thomas Mallory's fifteenth-century masterpiece, *Le Mort d'Arthur*. This was a retelling of the myth of King Arthur and his court, set in medieval England. It was reworked in verse by Tennyson, who dedicated the epic to Queen Victoria. Pre-Raphaelite artists such as Holman Hunt and Rossetti used themes from the Arthurian legends in their paintings. Sometimes there were crossovers, so that Tennyson's poem *The Lady of Shallot*, a spin-off from the Arthurian legends, was turned into a masterpiece of Pre-Raphaelite art.

Something very similar to the cult of Medievalism which swept Victorian Britain seems to be happening now in this country, driven by precisely similar advances in technology and just the same dislike of the modern world. The inspiration for many of those who long to turn the clock back is now to be found not in the medieval romances of Thomas Mallory, but rather a strange confection of images which seem to be drawn largely from the books of authors such as Enid Blyton and Richmal Crompton.

Just as the Victorians found that the world seemed to be turning a lot more quickly than it had when they were children, so too with today's middle-aged baby boomers. A man or woman who was 50 in the 1870s, when the transatlantic telegraph line began operations, could remember the days before steam trains and electrical communication. Everything really was moving faster for the Victorians and it wasn't always a pleasurable experience. The youngest of the baby boomers are now in their early 50s and will recall that when they were a little younger, sending a family snapshot to a relative in Australia was a pretty complicated, expensive and time-consuming business. One had to buy a film from the chemist's, take the photographs, go back to the chemist's with the film and have it developed and then wait a week or so before getting the pictures. After that, it was a question of getting an envelope, putting the photographs in and going down to the post office to send them to Australia. From taking the pictures until their receipt on the other side of the world would therefore take a minimum of about two weeks. This fortnight's delay has now been reduced to a fraction of a second, the time it takes to press 'send' and transmit a photograph just taken, all the way to the recipient in Australia or pretty much anywhere else in the world.

When the baby boomers were born, most people did not even have a telephone in their home. It was not until 1975 that the proportion of British homes with a telephone exceeded 50 per cent. Now, almost everybody carries with them their own personal telephone: wherever you are, you can be reached. Readers will probably not need to stretch their minds very much to supply another dozen or so examples of the way in which everything has speeded up enormously during the lives of the baby boomers.

Just as thoughtful Victorians sought refuge in the imaginary world of chivalrous knights and their ladies, so the baby boomers look back to their own mythical land which is so much more pleasing than the real one which they inhabit. It is a place of smiling, happy children, all of whom are slender and healthy. They leave their homes alone in the morning to go to school and return by themselves in the late afternoon. At weekends and during holidays, it is either warm and sunny or the world is covered in a blanket of picturesque snow and all the children can go tobogganing and build snowmen. In this charming age, there are no grey, drizzly evenings, where life drags and children are fed up with having to drift aimlessly round the streets, wishing that there was some other way of spending their time. Nor are there any real hazards for the children, as long as they are sure to be home for tea.

Of course, it is not only the baby boomers who have seen startling changes in the speed with which we conduct our lives; which explains perhaps why even younger people of 30 or so are keen to accept the version of the past which the baby boomers are peddling. Articles in newspapers and magazines extolling the joys of baby boomer childhood are often written by people in their 30s. Young people too have seen the digital revolution gather pace and change their lives in a hundred different ways. Let us take the case of a man or woman born in 1987, who is now 30 years of age. When these young adults started secondary school in 1998, the majority of them were living in homes without computers. At that time, only a third of British children lived in homes which had computers. Only a quarter of homes were then connected to the Internet and there were no smartphones. Facebook was not launched until 2004, when most of this generation had left school. At that time, there were no such things as Twitter or Youtube.

In short, it is not just the baby boomers who grew up in a very different world: 30-year-olds grew up themselves at a time before the digital revolution had really got going and much of what we today take for granted had not even been thought of. Today, these people are at the mercy of their smartphones and tablets, feeling obliged to check Twitter, Facebook or their emails at least a hundred times a day. Many feel trapped by this endless cycle of constantly needing to access the Internet, hence the growing popularity of the 'digital detox'.

The generation which followed the baby boomers are now finding that things have changed dramatically since they were children, and the pre-electronic era which the baby boomers describe, where they went out all day and nobody could contact them, appeals strongly to such people, who are aged roughly between 30 and 50. They feel that they only just missed the happiest era of all. Because we are still in the midst of the revolution in electronic communication, which is shaping our lives in so many different ways, there is a general uncertainty about the future; nobody knows how the Internet, virtual reality, social media and education will change in the coming years. The simple, healthy and uncomplicated lives which children are said to have enjoyed in the 1950s are calculated to strike a chord with people of this age. They can recall a time when all their friends were people known to them in real life and where coming home from work meant that you could relax with your family and not be pestered with work emails even while you ate your dinner. It is not surprising that they find the vision of the baby boomers' world attractive.

Whether this is the correct explanation, it is impossible to say. What is certain is that many of the initiatives aimed at improving the health, educational attainment and general character of the nation's children are predicated on the assumption that the 1950s were the best of times for children and that the more closely our children's lives are modelled on that period; the happier and healthier they will be.

We have looked at the childhood years of the baby boomers and found them wanting. Far from being a golden age for children, that period was really rather a dreary and hazardous one for children, with far more of them failing to survive to adulthood than is now the case. Their lives were in general a lot duller and lacking in interest than those of modern children. Baby boomer childhood has become mythologised though; to the extent that it is now taken as axiomatic that children's lives in the 1950s were far better than those of children in early 21st-century Britain. As long as this mistaken idea is limited to the reminiscences of old people, little harm is caused. When governments and professionals begin acting upon such false beliefs, as now regularly happens, it is time to stop and think about what is going on.

Bibliography

Blyton, Enid, *The Six Bad Boys*, London, Lutterworth Press, 1951.

Buchanan, Alexandrina, *Gothic Glories*, Norwich, Jarrold Publishing, 2005.

Cunningham, Hugh, *The Invention of Childhood*, London, BBC Books, 2006.

Furedi, Frank, *Paranoid Parenting: Abandon Your Anxieties and be a Good Parent*, London, Penguin Press, 2001.

Furedi, Frank, and Bristow, Jennie, *Licensed to Hug*, London, Civitas, 2010.

Gill, T., *No Fear: Growing Up in a Risk Averse Society*, London, Calouste Gulbenkian Foundation, 2007.

Guldberg, Helene, *Reclaiming Childhood; Freedom and Play in an Age of Fear*, Abingdon, Routledge, 2009.

Hennessy, Peter, *Having it so Good: Britain in the Fifties*, London, Penguin Books, 2006.

Horn, Pamela, *The Victorian and Edwardian Schoolchild* Gloucester, Alan Sutton Publishing, 1989.

Huntington, Robert, *The Nanny State*, London, Artnik, 2004.

Jones, Steve, *Capital Punishments*, Nottingham, Wicked Publications, 1992.

Kynaston, David, *Family Britain 1951-57*, London, Bloomsbury Publishing, 2009.

Kynaston, David, *Modernity Britain 1957-62*, London, Bloomsbury Publishing, 2015.

Ladybird Books, *Boys and Girls: A Ladybird Book of Childhood*, London, Ladybird Books, 2007.

Marshall, Arthur, *Girls Will be Girls*, London, Hamish Hamilton, 1974.

Opie, Peter, *Remember When*, London, Octopus Publishing, 1999.

Opie, Peter, *The 1950s Scrapbook*, London, New Cavendish Books, 2000.

Opie, Peter, *The 1960s Scrapbook*, London, New Cavendish Books, 2000.

Palmer, Sue, *Toxic Childhood: How the Modern World is Damaging our Children and What we can Do About It*, London, Orion, 2010.

Philips, Melanie, *All Must Have Prizes*, London, Little, Brown and Company, 1996.

Piper, H., and Stronach, I., *Don't Touch! The Educational Story of a Panic*, London, Routledge, 2008.

Pressley, Alison, *The 50s and 60s: The Best of Times*, London, Michael O'Mara Books, 2003.

Stack, Steve, *21st Century Dodos*, London, HarperCollins, 2011.

Sweet, Matthew, *Inventing the Victorians*, London, Faber & Faber, 2001.

Webb, Simon, *A 1960s East End Childhood*, Stroud, The History Press, 2012.

Webb, Simon, *A 1970s Teenager*, Stroud, The History Press, 2013.

Webb, Simon, *The Best days of Our Lives; School Life in Post-War Britain*, Stroud, The History Press, 2013.

Wertham, Frederic, *Seduction of the Innocent*, New York, Rinehart & Company, 1954.

Willmott, Peter, *Adolescent Boys of East London*, London, Routledge & Kegan Paul, 1966.

Index